# RECIPES THAT WORK

# RECIPES THAT WORK

—PATRICK DRAKE—

## MORE THAN 100 STEP-BY-STEP RECIPES & TECHNIQUES

MITCHELL BEAZLEY

An Hachette UK Company
www.hachette.co.uk

First published in Great Britain in 2018 by
Mitchell Beazley, a division of Octopus
Publishing Group Ltd
Carmelite House
50 Victoria Embankment
London EC4Y 0DZ
www.octopusbooks.co.uk

ISBN 978-1-78472-465-8

A CIP catalogue record for this book is
available from the British Library.

Printed and bound in China

10 9 8 7 6 5 4 3

Publisher: Alison Starling
Senior Editor: Pauline Bache
Art Directors: Yasia Williams-Leedham
   and Geoff Fennell
Senior Production Controller:
   Allison Gonsalves

Photographer: Jason Ingram
Photography Assistant: George Bales
Food Stylist: Sian Henley
Food Styling Assistant: Megan Davies
Props Stylist: Agathe Gits

HelloFresh Art Directors:
   Björn Welter and Maria Coelho
HelloFresh Icons and Illustrations:
   Michel Arencibia and Susana Mac Loughlin

Publisher's notes:
Fresh herb amounts are specified in
tablespoons to give an easy visual reference.
Please note for shopping purposes, that none
of the tablespoon amounts mentioned are
more than a small packet of fresh herbs.

Ovens should be preheated to the specific
temperature – if using a fan-assisted oven,
follow the manufacturer's instructions for
adjusting the time and the temperature.

This book includes dishes made with nuts and
nut derivatives. It is advisable for customers
with known allergic reactions to nuts and nut
derivatives, and those who may be potentially
vulnerable to these allergies, such as pregnant
and nursing mothers, invalids, the elderly,
babies and children, to avoid dishes made with
nuts and nut oils. It is also prudent to check
the labels of ready-made ingredients for the
possible inclusion of nut derivatives.

Vegetarians should look for the 'V' symbol on
a cheese to ensure it is made with vegetarian
rennet. There are vegetarian forms of
Parmesan, feta, Cheddar, Cheshire, Red
Leicester, dolcelatte and many goats' cheeses,
among others.

# CONTENTS

# THIS ISN'T A COFFEE-TABLE BOOK

I didn't want to create a book that would just look pretty on a shelf. I want this to become the most loved, reliable, sauce-spattered, page-folded go-to in your kitchen. Every decision in creating the book is based around making your dinners delicious and fresh and making your life simple. From dividing the chapters simply by protein, to giving you the hacks and tricks to get dinner on the table fast and without fuss. It can be a beginner's guide for the uninitiated or a source of quick inspiration to the seasoned cook.

**We asked. And our customers spoke (a lot!)**
When HelloFresh first started, we developed recipes entirely by instinct. Our kind of cooking has always been hearty, honest, solid home-cooked food. No haute-cuisine drizzles of this and Jenga stacks of that.

But pretty soon we started sending out a questionnaire with each recipe to ask our customers to give us really honest feedback.

Imagine a chef in a restaurant trying to knock out dinner, whilst everyone lines up to tell him what they thought of the food. We had to grow a pretty thick skin, quickly.

**The most tested recipes in the world.**
That questionnaire was a game-changer for us and, really, it's the basis of this whole book. Now we get hundreds of thousands of replies and we use all of those scores and opinions to rank our recipes and help create the new ones. Having started out with one chef, we've now got a team headed up by André and Mimi and, under the watchful eye of Lizzie, each recipe gets meticulously tested in our cooking school before it goes out. The end result? They're probably the most tested dinners in the world.

So that's what we've put together here: a selection of the all-time customer favourite recipes, tried and tested by hundreds of thousands of HelloFresh customers.

Fancy a quick, delicious fix at 8pm on a Wednesday? You can have our Prawn & Prosciutto Linguine (*see* page 118) on the table in the time it takes to cook the pasta. If you want a bit of inspiration without any fuss, give our Sweetcorn Fritters a spin (*see* page 40). And if you need to seriously impress your friends at the weekend then it's all about our Confit Duck Lasagne on page 212. Whatever life throws at you, we've got you covered.

# A BIT OF HELLOFRESH HISTORY

**I love the naivety of youth.**

In January 2012 we started HelloFresh in the UK. We were excited. We'd decided to 'democratise good food', we were going to, 'change the way people cook and eat. Forever.' The reality was far from those grandiose dreams.

(To give you the background, the big idea behind HelloFresh is to take away all the reasons why people aren't cooking great homemade dinners from scratch. We send recipes, together with a chilled box of the exact ingredients you need to cook those recipes, straight to your doorstep. Now back to the story…)

We made our first deliveries two weeks after we decided to set up the company. There we stood in my living room in Old Street, with a few recipes I had knocked together and a trolley of ingredients we'd 'sourced' from the various supermarkets in the neighbourhood. We chopped up bits of Parmesan and wrapped them in clingfilm, printed our (Clipart) logo at the local print shop and packed ten paper bags. Next we delivered them on the train to the only people who had heard of us: our parents. By the end of the day, we were exhausted, pretty happy with our progress, but wondered, if the company grew, how we'd ever manage to pack fifty bags of shopping in a day.

**I'm not sure any of us foresaw where we'd end up.**

The next few months (and years) were a frenzied blur. There were five of us at the start and each person represented an entire department of the company (the person who was nearest the phone when it rang also became customer care for that call). I was in charge of recipe development, but since we couldn't afford a photographer at the time, I bought myself an old camera, watched some YouTube videos and became our photographer too.

**A marathon…and a sprint.**

From the very start we wanted our recipes to be so much more than beautiful photos with blocks of text underneath it. We wanted to break down the cooking process and teach people how to nail it every single time with step-by-step photos and really methodical instructions. The upshot? Every five minutes whilst cooking a recipe I'd have to run out of the kitchen with the chopping board/ saucepan/you name it, put it on my living room floor, take a photo, then run back into the kitchen to keep cooking. It was a marathon.

While I would dream up the recipes, my good friend Luke was the one who actually had to make them happen. He was in charge of ordering the ingredients, getting them delivered to our new warehouse (which was actually a bit of unused space in a friend's boat shed), packing them and arranging deliveries. The poor lad didn't have it easy at the beginning. I remember he had a long list of potential suppliers and he'd sit there every day optimistically calling them and explaining why they should be part of our 'revolutionary' movement. The click of a phone being hung up became the soundtrack to his day, until a few people (big shout to Mike 'The Guru' Thorpe down at Covent Garden market) decided to get on board.

**Our only meeting room also doubled as our spice-packing room.**

No supplier volunteered to pack our spices into individual teaspoon-sized pots though, so our only meeting room also doubled as a production line. Whenever we had an external meeting, it became all-hands-on-deck to clear out all the spices to create some semblance of professionalism. We never could get rid of the smell of garam masala though.

Things have changed a bit since those 'frontier' days. At the date of publishing this book HelloFresh is sending out millions of meals a month across the world, so that youthful optimism wasn't misplaced. I hope, in some small way, we can change the way you cook and eat forever too ;-)

HelloFresh UK
co-founders,
Patrick Drake and
Luke Grob

A flat wooden spatula for turning things like fish fillets

A fine grater for zesting citrus fruit or grating hard cheeses like Parmesan

A few wooden spoons

Tongs for flipping things in the pan without burning your fingers

A vegetable peeler

A small pair of sharp scissors

# SETTING UP YOUR KITCHEN

Don't have a £500 food processor and a spiraliser? Don't worry. People were knocking out great dinners for centuries before all that stuff existed and our recipes only need the bare minimum of equipment. Back in the day, if we couldn't cook every dinner with a couple of pots and pans in our cramped little kitchen, then it wouldn't make the cut. We still always aim to keep everything simple. Here are all the basics we used then and now.

*If you can stretch your budget a little, I've put an asterisk (*) next to the things you might want to spend a bit more on. Ultimately, you do pay for quality, and certain bits of equipment can last for decades if they're good and you look after them.

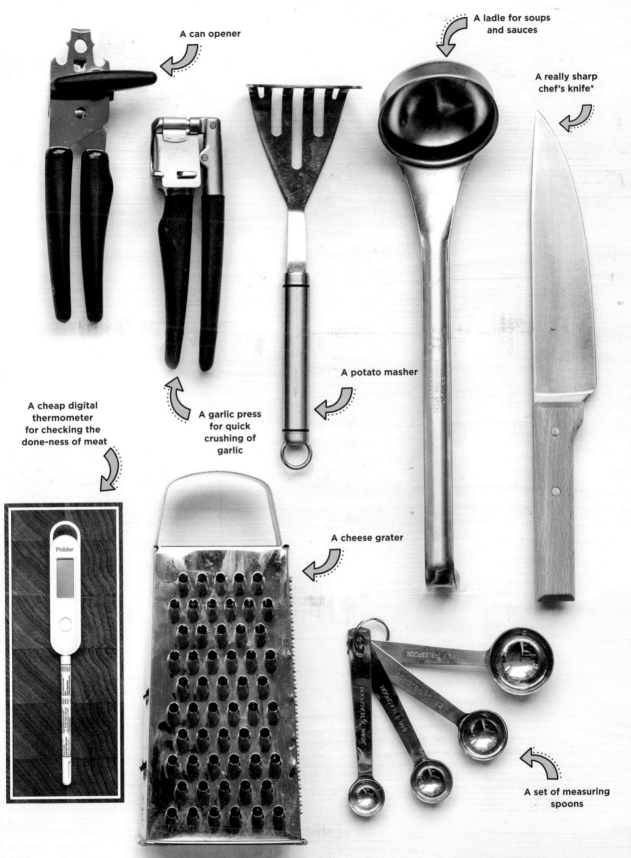

A can opener

A ladle for soups
and sauces

A really sharp
chef's knife*

A potato masher

A cheap digital
thermometer
for checking the
done-ness of meat

A garlic press
for quick
crushing of
garlic

A cheese grater

Polder

A set of measuring
spoons

A colander for draining vegetables and pasta, and a fine mesh sieve for straining bits out of sauces

Baking paper and clingfilm

At least two baking trays for roasting meat and vegetables

It's worth investing in a couple of good quality medium-sized pots and a non-stick frying pan with heavy bottoms as they're tougher and won't burn your food so easily*

A measuring jug for measuring out liquids

A bench scraper to help you pick up scraps or things you've chopped up

A chopping board for meat and preferably another one for chopping veg

An ovenproof dish for things like casseroles*

A small and a large mixing bowl for...well... mixing stuff

A few tea towels

# STORE CUPBOARD ESSENTIALS

These pages do what they say on the tin. Armed with these basics, you'll always be able to knock up something quick and tasty for dinner. And because all the store cupboard staples are long lasting, it's only the things like protein and fresh veg that you'll need to add into the mix.

REGULAR (AKA 'LIGHT')
OLIVE OIL FOR COOKING

GOOD-QUALITY OLIVE
OIL FOR DRESSINGS

**SEASONING:** black pepper, sea salt flakes,
table salt

**VINEGARS:** balsamic, red wine vinegar, white wine
vinegar, rice vinegar

PLAIN FLOUR

CORNFLOUR

**STOCK POTS OR STOCK CUBES**
(vegetable, chicken, beef, fish)

**DRIED HERBS:** oregano, thyme, rosemary, Provençal
mixed herbs, Italian mixex herbs

**SPICES:** ground cumin, ground coriander, smoked
paprika, mild paprika, turmeric, curry powders,
ground cinnamon, nutmeg, chilli powder or flakes,
fajita/Mexican spice mix

TABASCO SAUCE

WORCESTERSHIRE SAUCE

MAYONNAISE

KETCHUP

SOY SAUCE

KETJAP MANIS
(SWEET SOY SAUCE)

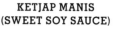

FISH SAUCE

SWEET CHILLI SAUCE

TINNED TOMATOES

TOMATO PURÉE

TOMATO PASSATA

COCONUT MILK

CAPERS

RED KIDNEY BEANS

COOKED LENTILS

RED SPLIT LENTILS

**RICE:** arborio risotto rice, basmati
rice (brown and white)

EGG NOODLES

**PASTA:** Penne or rigatoni, spaghetti or tagliatelle

**MUSTARD:** Dijon, wholegrain mustard

## (ALSO USEFUL TO KEEP IN
## THE FRIDGE)

CRÈME FRAÎCHE

GREEK YOGHURT

NATURAL YOGHURT

EGGS

DOUBLE CREAM

BUTTER

# PREVENTING FOOD WASTE

The big idea behind HelloFresh is that we find the ingredients, portion them out and send you exactly what you need for your dinner. Only need one teaspoon of smoked paprika? No problem, that's all we'll send. Recipe calls for two carrots? We won't send you any more. The best bit about that way of doing things is how much food waste we're cutting down. There's also a bunch of simple things you can do at home that'll help cut down on throwing food out. The upside? A clear conscience and a healthier bank balance.

### ONLY BUY WHAT YOU NEED

Whenever possible, buy the exact amount of ingredients you need for a recipe. Try to find shops where you can buy single carrots, potatoes, onions and other fresh produce instead of using large packets. You'll be amazed how this step alone cuts back on kilos of chucked-out veggies.

### FREEZE

Sometimes buying in bulk makes sense from a cost perspective, but there's always the risk you won't use everything before it goes off. If you're buying packets of freezable ingredients (like meat) and you're not using everything that week, stick the excess in freezer bags, label it with the date and freeze it until you need it. Bread is another great contender, as you can stick it straight in the toaster or just defrost it for a few hours before you need to use it. Even things like spinach and soft fruits (e.g. overripe bananas) can be frozen and then whizzed up to make delicious smoothies.

### FIRST IN, FIRST OUT

Have you ever taken something out of the fridge and been unsure whether it had gone off or not, so decided to put it back in the fridge until you *really* know it's gone off? Don't worry, you're not the only one! The best way to arrange your fridge (and your cupboards) is by bringing the oldest items to the front and putting the newer ones to the back. That way you'll see the older stuff first and hopefully use it in time.

### STORAGE

When you're putting things like dairy, cooked foods and meat in the fridge, be sure to wrap them up tightly in clingfilm or in an airtight plastic box. Half-eaten tins of food should be emptied into a bowl and wrapped. For dry items, like pasta, flour, spices and nuts, get yourself a bunch of glass jars with those rubber seals and clip lids. They'll keep things fresh for longer, and if you use one of those old-fashioned label guns to name each one, they'll look pretty great too.

### GET FRITTATA-ING

Spanish omelettes, frittatas, bubble 'n' squeak. Whichever country you visit there's usually a local dish that revamps their leftovers. To cook a frittata take leftover cooked veggies and meat, mix it up with a few whisked eggs and then fry it off on both sides in your frying pan. Perfect with that half bag of salad you weren't sure how to use up.

### THE PERFECT PORTION

Just because a packet of rice or pasta comes in a particular size, it doesn't mean that it's the right amount for your meal. Keep an eye on what you're throwing away after meals and pretty soon you'll get a sense of how to adjust your portions to a size where there are no more leftovers. That said, if the leftovers are something that can be eaten the next day for lunch or a revamped dinner, everyone's a winner.

Preventing food waste feels like a small daily victory and there's lots of information out there on composting, pickling, how to best store different foods and much more besides. We're partnered with Love Food, Hate Waste and you can get all sorts of tips and tricks on their website at www.lovefoodhatewaste.com.

# COOKING TIPS THAT WORK

When we started writing our recipes we were determined not to be like so many of the cookbooks we'd read. Terms like 'butterfly', 'a glug', 'a splash', 'a pinch' and 'caramelise' may be obvious to the people writing the books, but they're not that helpful to the uninitiated. The balance was to be as methodical and clear as possible, but without straying into patronising the reader. I hope we have managed that.

Instead of saying 'butterfly' the chicken, we'll explain how to butterfly it. And words like 'brunoise' and 'julienne' are banned in the HelloFresh Kitchen (let's all just relax...it's a carrot stick). For those starting out we're creating efficient habits, whilst more experienced cooks can skim through the detail more quickly.

We have tried and tested (with our customers) the techniques that follow literally thousands of times. They'll speed up your kitchen game and make sure you get the best results every time.

## HOW TO HOLD A KNIFE

**The majority of your chopping will be done with a chef's knife. Our preferred length is somewhere between 15cm and 20cm and, since it's arguably the most important piece of kitchen equipment you'll own, it's worth spending a little more money on a good one. I'd also recommend buying your knife in a shop rather than online so you can try a few out and get some advice.**

**1.** To hold the knife, pinch the blade between the index finger and thumb of your knife hand, just next to the handle.

**2.** Your index finger should be tucked under so that there's no chance of it getting near the sharp edge.

**3.** Your remaining three fingers should curl around the handle so that it's resting snugly against your palm.

This grip will feel a bit alien at first, but after a while it will become second nature (I promise). Whilst we're on the subject, don't be tempted to put your index finger along the top of the blade as it gives you less control and could lead to an injury.

# HOW TO USE YOUR KNIFE

Good chopping technique is definitely not about speed. It's about accuracy and keeping all of your digits intact. Here's the lowdown…

**1.** Whatever you're chopping, the first thing to do is make sure that the ingredient is stable on the chopping board, rather than rolling about. For larger items, the best way to do this is create a flat edge on the ingredient and use this edge to rest on.

**2.** Next is 'the claw'(!). When you hold the ingredient down, curl your fingers under so that there's no chance the tips of your fingers can

get nipped by your knife. Experienced choppers tend to use the knuckles on their index and middle fingers to rest the knife against as a guide…though if that feels a little too close to the edge, you can always just keep your fingers a few centimetres back from where the chopping happens. This may mean your accuracy isn't quite as good, but nobody is going to criticise you if your 'brunoise' (carrot cubes) aren't perfect.

# THE SLICING MOTION

We explain different knife techniques throughout the book, but the one you will use most often is a slicing motion.

**1.** Start with the end of your knife touching the chopping board and your hand raised upwards (to allow space under the blade for your ingredient).

**2.** To slice the ingredient, push your knife hand downwards **at the same time as you move it smoothly forwards**. The knife should always be in contact with the board throughout the movement.

**3.** At the end of the movement (once you have made the slice), bring your knife hand upwards **at the same time as you move it smoothly backwards**.

I promise not to use bold type again, but it's really important to do the down/forwards and the up/backwards moves at the same time. You'll notice that your knife hand actually goes around in a circle when you've got the movement just right.

# KEEPING YOUR KNIFE SHARP

I heard a wilderness survival expert once say, 'Look after your knife and your knife will look after you.' Full disclosure: I wasn't in the wilderness, it was on the telly.

Generally speaking, a more European-style knife, rather than a Japanese knife, will be a little easier to keep sharp, since Japanese knives have a more acute angle on their cutting edge.

When you're using your knife, never scrape it across the top of your chopping board to move ingredients as this will make it go blunt quickly.

When you put the knife away, either stick it in a knife block, put a guard around it before it goes in the drawer or just wrap a tea towel around it (i.e. tuck your knife in for the night).

To keep the edge on the blade you can use a metal or ceramic rod (called a 'steel'), but the easiest way is to use a roller through which you simply drag the knife to 'hone' the edge.

# FINELY CHOPPING VS ROUGHLY CHOPPING

The same amount of parsley roughly chopped and finely chopped

Finely chopped onion compared to finely chopped garlic

This is another wonderfully vague term that's used a lot in cookbooks, but never really defined. To be honest, my definition isn't exactly from a dictionary, more from personal experience, but it's worked for every recipe I've cooked.

'Finely chopped' is often used interchangeably with the term 'finely diced', but both mean you're chopping the ingredient into pieces that are ½cm or less. Finely chopped/diced onions are usually around ½cm, but when the term is used for herbs or garlic you may even go down to 1 or 2mm (you can see how to do this on pages 21–23).

Generally speaking, the stronger the flavour of an ingredient, the finer you'll end up chopping it. That means when you're eating the dish you won't end up with a big, overpowering chunk in your mouth.

'Roughly chopped' is a slightly more haphazard term. If I was roughly chopping an onion, the size would be around 2cm, and if it were herbs, the size would be just under 1cm. In our recipes you'll usually see a photograph to show the size and pretty quickly you'll get an instinct for what's needed.

One universal rule is that whether you are finely chopping/dicing or roughly chopping, make sure that everything is the same size so that it all cooks in the same amount of time.

Throughout the book we've referred to fresh herb amounts in tablespoons. The idea is to give you an easy visual reference and train your instincts for the volume of herbs needed. A note for when you're shopping: none of the tablespoon amounts mentioned are more than a small packet of fresh herbs.

## WHAT TYPE OF COOKING OIL IS BEST?

'Horses for courses' as my grandad would say. The type of cooking oil you use depends on the flavour you want, the temperature at which you're cooking and the nutritional profile. From day one at HelloFresh we always said to people that once they had a box of our recipes 'the only thing you'll need is salt, pepper and olive oil', so nearly all of our recipes simply used olive oil (even Asian dishes). You can use a flavourless oil like rapeseed if you prefer, or coconut oil for certain dishes like curry, but you'll find that a light 'frying' olive oil does the trick nine times out of ten. Just don't tell the puritans!

## WHAT IS A 'PINCH OF SALT'?

**Ahhh, the million pound question. I'm going to drive a stake in the ground and say that this is probably the most vague and under-explained term in cooking. But no longer!**

Reading through recipes you'll most likely come across this wily phrase in three guises: 'a small pinch', 'a pinch' and 'a good pinch'. I'd say that those terms roughly translate as follows:

'A small pinch': less than ¼ tsp (the amount you can pinch between thumb and index finger)

'A pinch': ¼ tsp (the amount you can pinch between thumb, index and middle finger)

'A good pinch': ½ tsp (the amount you can pinch between thumb and all fingers)

For the sake of clarity we've gone with these teaspoon measurements throughout the book so that you can get the seasoning just right. That said, the salt level in a dish is a matter of personal taste and the best thing you can do is taste the food throughout the cooking process and add more or less according to your own preference.

We always use flaked sea salt in the dishes themselves and lower-quality table salt only when seasoning pasta water or water for boiling potatoes.

## A NOTE ON INGREDIENTS PREPARATION

At HelloFresh one of the things we set out to do is make the cooking process more efficient.

The method for preparing ingredients is detailed in the ingredients list for each recipe and we'll explain the best timing to do that prep in the recipe method itself.

The majority of techniques for ingredient prep are explained in the front of the book and sometimes we've added a bit more detail into the recipe as well.

Prep times in each recipe are the total time to get dinner on the table, including the time it takes for prep work and chopping.

You'll notice that we go into a fair bit of detail in each recipe to make each step clear, but if you're an experienced cook you may wish to skip over the detail.

 ## CITRUS FRUITS: ZEST

**Zesting limes and oranges into things like salad dressings and sauces is a great way to add a beautiful hit of zesty fragrance and flavour. Here's how…**

First off get yourself a zester. It's essentially a very fine cheese grater, but a little less unwieldy and the result will be a nice fine zest.

Grate the citrus fruit against the zester, but be sure that you only take off the top colourful layer. Once you reach the white part underneath, stop grating/zesting as this part is the bitter-tasting pith.

# GARLIC: GRATING, FINELY CHOPPING, CRUSHING & MASHING

Garlic is an ingredient you'll see a lot, as it forms the base flavour of dishes from around the globe. Garlic cloves come in different sizes, so when we say 'a garlic clove' you can assume it weighs about 6g. Grating, crushing and chopping will all yield pretty similar results, so take your pick. Mashing will create a very fine paste and is good where you're using the garlic raw in a dressing.

### GRATING

To grate a clove of garlic simply peel off the skin and then grate it against the finest side of your cheese grater or against a zester.

### FINELY CHOPPING

**1.** To finely chop the garlic, peel the clove then rest the flat of your knife on top of it. Give it a whack with the heel of your hand to crush it and then chop, chop, chop until the pieces are around 1mm small.

**2.** The easiest way to do this is rest the tip of your knife on the board as a pivot point, place your fingers flat on top of the knife and then move up and down.

### CRUSHING

To crush garlic you don't even need to peel the clove. Just stick it in the garlic press and give it a good squeeze.

### MASHING

Lastly, to extract maximum flavour, you can mash the garlic. Peel and finely chop the clove, sprinkle over a little bit of salt (less than ¼ tsp) and drag the sharp edge of your knife continuously towards you over the garlic, until you have a soft mulch (a 'purée').

# PEPPERS: STICKS & DICE

I'm not going to claim this is the definitive way to chop a pepper, but it's the way I find quickest and, for some reason I can't explain, the most satisfying.

**1.** Turn the pepper on its side and slice off the very top and the very bottom.

**2.** To remove the core stand the pepper up and put a lengthways cut right down one side, then open it up and run your knife along the inside to remove the seeds.

**3.** To make sticks simply slice the pepper lengthways according to the size you need for the recipe. Pepper sticks are great for stir-fry dishes.

**4.** If your recipe needs dice, take the sticks and chop them widthways. Finely diced raw peppers (½ cm cubes) are delicious in a salad.

# CARROT: STICKS & DICE

Like the garlic before, you'll get plenty of practice doing this, since diced carrot (combined with diced onion) forms the base flavour of so many dishes.

**1.** Start by 'peeling and stabilising' the carrot. Place the carrot on the chopping board and slice lengthways along one edge to create a flat surface. Rest it on the flat side and slice along a second side and then a third to create a (rough) square shape.

**2.** To create carrot sticks, rest your fingers on the remaining rounded edge to hold the carrot down and slice lengthways. The width between each slice will determine the size of the sticks and the cubes you end up with. Stack the slices on top of each other and then slice them lengthways again to create sticks.

**3.** If your recipe needs dice, line all of the sticks in the same direction and use your fingers in a claw to hold them all together, keeping your fingers far enough back from the edge so that there's no chance of nipping them.

**4.** Chop the carrot sticks widthways. When a recipe says 'finely dice' it usually means that the cubes should be around ½cm thick.

# CHILLI: DESEEDING & FINELY CHOPPING

The larger chillis you commonly see in shops aren't that hot, but if you want to reduce their heat, then scrape out the seeds. Most importantly, once you've handled a chilli, wash your hands really well: chilli finger in the eye isn't nice!

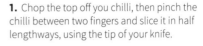

**1.** Chop the top off you chilli, then pinch the chilli between two fingers and slice it in half lengthways, using the tip of your knife.

**2.** To remove the seeds from the chilli, press your finger down on one end to hold it steady and then scrape the seeds away from you using your knife. If you fancy planting your own chilli tree, put the seeds in a bit of soil and pretty soon you won't need to buy any more chillies.

**3.** To create chilli batons (i.e. thin slices), thinly slice the chilli lengthways, very carefully, so that each slice is a few mm thick at most.

**4.** For finely chopped chilli, chop all of your batons widthways. Your cubes should be a couple of mm thick.

# GINGER: PEELING & CHOPPING

If one cooking technique could top the league table for customer favourites then this would be it. Ginger is fantastic as the base flavour for Asian stir-fry recipes and curries, and with this technique you'll minimise waste and learn how to spread the flavour evenly through your dish.

**1.** Start by peeling the skin from the ginger. Rather than use a peeler or a knife, hold the knob of ginger in one hand and then use the edge of a teaspoon in the other hand to peel away the skin. (Move onto steps 2 and 3 to chop the ginger or, if you're in a rush, you can skip these steps and simply grate the peeled ginger using the fine side of a cheese grater or zester.)

**2.** If you're planning to chop the ginger finely, then you can kickstart the process by crushing it first. Place the flat side of your knife on top of the ginger and then press down firmly to crush it.

**3.** To chop ginger really finely press the tip of your knife onto the chopping board and place your fingers flat on top of the knife. Using the tip as a pivot point (i.e. do not let the tip leave the board) move the knife up and down, controlling the speed and movement of the knife using both hands to chop, chop, chop backwards and forwards until you have fine dice.

# LEEKS (& OTHER LONG VEG): DISCS, HALF MOONS & DICE

Leeks, spring onions, celery...this technique covers them all. Chop your way through a few bunches of celery and you'll have your technique down in no time.

## PREPPING

For leeks (and other long veg such as spring onions and green beans) there'll often be some dry ends or a root. Trim these off first.

## DISCS

Simply slice the vegetable widthways to the thickness you'd like. For most recipes that will usually be around ½cm.

## HALF MOONS

**1.** Slice in half lengthways and rest each half on its flat edge.

**2.** Now simply slice the halved vegetable widthways.

## DICE

**1.** Slice the vegetable lengthways into ½ cm strips. When I'm thinly slicing a long vegetable I find the easiest (and safest) way to stabilise it on the board is to pinch it between two fingers, then run the tip of the knife through it to cut it in half. This is particularly handy for celery.

**2.** Then just turn the slices widthways and chop it into ½cm dice.

# ONION: HALF MOONS & DICE

They say practice makes perfect and you'll be getting plenty of that with this technique, since onions form the base flavour of so many dishes. Remember, it's not about speed, it's about keeping all of your fingers.

### PEEL & HALVE

Chop the very top off but leave the root intact (this will hold it together). Rest on the flat top, slice in half lengthways and pull away the outer layer.

### HALF MOONS

Rest the peeled onion flat on the board and slice it thinly (around ½cm) widthways. These are your half moons.

### DICE

**1.** Lay half the onion flat on the board and slice through it lengthways (the wider the slices the bigger the 'dice'). Don't slice all the way through the root as this will hold it all together.

**2.** Now chop the onion widthways to create little cubes. For most dishes you'll want to space the slices around ½cm apart (which is often called 'finely diced').

# SWEET & REGULAR POTATOES: WEDGES & DICE

Sweet potatoes are one of the superstars of the vegetable world and for nearly all HelloFresh recipes we simply give them a wash, but leave that tasty, nutritious skin on. They're a little tougher than most veggies, so make sure you have a sharp chef's knife and be careful of your fingers.

## WEDGES

**1.** Trim the knobbly top and bottom off the sweet potato, then slice the sweet potato in half lengthways.

**2.** Rest each half flat on the chopping board and then, using your knife at an angle, slice your wedges around 2cm thick. If you're having trouble getting the knife through the potato then make sure it's stable on the board, place your fingers flat on top of the knife and push downwards with your weight. Keeping your fingers on top keeps them safe and gives you more force.

## DICE

**1.** Trim the knobbly top and bottom off the sweet potato, then slice off a thin lengthways layer to make a stable flat edge. Rest that flat side on the board, then slice it lengthways into strips (around 1–2cm thick). Take the strips and rest them on a flat side for stability, then slice them lengthways into sticks.

**2.** Now turn the sticks widthways and chop to the size that you want. Make sure they're all roughly the same size so that they cook evenly.

# CHICKEN BREASTS: BUTTERFLYING & TENDERISING

Butterflying and tenderising chicken breasts brings down their cooking time and, texture-wise, it works really well when you'd rather have a more delicate, thin piece of meat in your dish. We tend to use this technique for salads, breaded chicken or just when we want to get dinner on the table a bit quicker.

**1.** Lay the chicken breast flat on your chopping board and place your hand flat on top. Use your knife to slice into the breast from the side.

**2.** As your knife begins to slice through the breast, open it up like a book and use the tip of your knife blade to keep slicing through. Leave a little bit still attached at the side (like the spine of the book) to keep both halves of the breast together.

**3.** Tenderising can be pretty cathartic. Place a bit of clingfilm on your chopping board, put the chicken breast on top, then cover with another piece of clingfilm.

Now whack the chicken breast for all you're worth until it's around ½–1cm thick (depending on what you need for the particular recipe).

# HOW TO BOIL WATER (SERIOUSLY)

When I asked people about the cooking terms that confused them most, a lot of people said words like 'simmer', 'poach' and 'vigorous boil' could do with a bit of explaining. This might not be the most thrilling cooking lesson, but it'll make all the difference to the end results…

**POACHING** When your water is steaming but the surface is still, it's at a poaching temperature. This is the temperature you'll use for poaching eggs, or if you want to very gently and slowly cook meat or vegetables for a soft, moist finish.

**SIMMERING** At a simmering temperature the water is steaming, the surface of the water is rippling slightly and you might see the occasional bubble float up. Simmering is another low and slow cooking temperature that you might use to gradually thicken up a sauce, whilst deepening its flavours.

**GENTLE BOIL** Once your water is at a gentle boil it will have bubbles continually rising up from the bottom, though not so many that you can't see the ingredients under the water. You would use this temperature when you want to cook something relatively quickly, but without breaking it (like new potatoes).

**ROLLING BOIL** A rolling, hard or vigorous boil is the maximum temperature, where so many bubbles are rising from the bottom of the pan that the top of the water is frothy. You would use this temperature for tougher ingredients like dry pasta (since the bubbles will also stop the pasta sticking together) and brown rice.

# PERFECT RICE EVERY TIME

This technique has been honed to perfection over the years, so we're fairly confident it'll do what it says on the tin: 'perfect rice, every time'.

**1.** For two people (double, triple or quadruple all quantities for more) bring 300ml of water to a gentle boil with ¼ tsp of salt. Tip in 150g of white basmati rice.

**2.** Put a tightly fitting lid on the pan and leave it on a medium heat for 10 mins.

When the 10 mins are up, remove the pan from the heat and leave it for 10 mins, but do not peek under the lid or lift it up until the full 20 mins are up.

**3.** Once the rice has finished cooking in its own steam, fluff it up using a fork and you're good to go.

 # PERFECT PASTA

Throw it in the water, 10 mins, job done, right? Not quite. Italians are very particular when it comes to cooking their favourite staple. Here's what you need to know.

**1.** For pasta for two people (around 200g) bring at least 2 litres of water to a rapid boil with 1 tbsp of salt (never use oil in the water). It sounds like a lot of salt but only a small amount will sink into the pasta.

**2.** Once the water is vigorously boiling, add in the pasta and stir it around until the water comes back to the boil. The reason for the stirring is to stop the pasta from sticking together. Once the water is boiling, the bubbles will move the pasta enough to stop this happening.

**3.** Cook the pasta until it is 'al dente'. This Italian phrase means 'to the tooth' and it's the point at which the pasta is cooked through but has a very slight bit of firmness left in the middle. Check the cooking time on the packet as a guide. Drain and serve immediately.

For fresh pasta you'll only cook it for around 4 mins, but as different types vary, be sure to test it every minute. I tend to have a less vigorous boil for things like fresh ravioli or tortellini (and don't overcrowd the pot) as I don't want them to break open.

# THE PERFECT 'DONE-NESS' OF MEAT & FISH

**Bypass years of training with this one simple gadget**

One of the trickier parts of cooking is knowing when meat is perfectly cooked. Under-cooked, it could cause a food hygiene situation, over-cooked and your meat will end up tough as old boots. Chefs have all sorts of techniques for gauging the 'done-ness' of meat, but they're usually learned after a lot of practice and can still be inaccurate.

The best way to get perfect meat every time is to buy yourself an inexpensive meat thermometer. You just stick the spike into the deepest part of the meat and instantly it will let you know what's going on inside.

Technically, these are the temperatures to which you should take your meat to (and hold that temperature for 2 minutes) in order to know they are safely cooked.

| | |
|---|---|
| Beef, lamb, veal (steak, chops and roasts) | 63°C |
| Chicken, turkey, duck, goose, stuffing | 74°C |
| Pork | 72°C |
| Minced lamb, veal, beef, pork | 72°C |
| Minced chicken and turkey | 74°C |
| **Fish** – cook it until the meat goes from a slightly translucent colour to opaque | 72°C |
| **Prawns, lobster, crab** – cook until they go from a translucent colour to opaque (e.g. prawns go from grey to pink) | 72°C |
| Leftovers, casseroles and stews | 74°C |
| **Eggs** – cook until the whites go from translucent to white | 63–70°C |

## 'RARE', 'MEDIUM RARE', 'WELL DONE'...EXCUSE ME?

Many people prefer to eat meat such as beef, lamb, veal and fish below the recommended 'safe' temperature for a more juicy, tender mouthful. Whilst I'd never do this with poultry, I do think if you've got a very fresh piece of steak it's better to eat it at medium rare so that you get the full, juicy flavour.

Opposite is a list of different cooking temperatures for different finishes:

| | |
|---|---|
| **extra-rare or blue**<br>very red and cold | 46–49°C |
| **rare**<br>cold red centre, soft to the touch | 52–55°C |
| **medium rare**<br>warm red centre, firmer | 55–60°C |
| **medium**<br>pink and firm | 60–65°C |
| **medium well**<br>small bit of pink in the middle | 65–69°C |
| **well done**<br>greyish-brown colour inside and out | 71°C+ |

## A NOTE ON RAW MEAT SAFETY

When preparing raw meat (in particular raw chicken and pork-based products), always practise good hygiene to reduce the risk of contaminating your hands, cooking equipment and other ingredients. Always wash your hands well with soap and water after handling raw meat and don't reuse any kitchen equipment that has been used for raw meat on other ingredients without giving the equipment a good wash first. It's a good idea to have a couple of chopping boards with one that you always use for veg and one that you always use for meat, to avoid getting them mixed up when you're in the middle of cooking.

Finally, when cooking poultry, pork and seafood, always ensure that it's fully cooked in the middle before serving. For poultry and pork this means that there is no pink flesh in the thickest part of the meat, while for seafood this means that the flesh has turned opaque all the way through the middle.

# VEGETARIAN
## -DISHES-

# CAJUN (OR MEXICAN) HALLOUMI BURGERS
## – WITH CHUNKY SWEET POTATO CHIPS–

For this recipe the secret's in the sauce. The garlic sauce to be precise. Rather than simply chopping the garlic into little bits, you'll be using the flat of your knife to make a paste instead. It's a bit cheffy, but when you taste the end result you'll never go back. Here the halloumi is rubbed with a Cajun or Mexican spice mix to zing it up. Be prepared to fend off envious meat-eaters.

**READY IN 30 MINS**

**SERVES 2**

## Ingredients

- 600g sweet potato, 2cm thick wedges
- olive oil
- 1 vine tomato, ½cm slices
- 2 garlic cloves, mashed
- 2 tsp Cajun (or Mexican) spice mix
- 1 block halloumi cheese, 1cm slices
- 150g soured cream
- 2 brioche buns
- 1 baby gem lettuce, thinly shredded
- salt and black pepper

## Here's how...

**1** Preheat your oven to 220°C/Gas Mark 7. Wash and chop your **sweet potato** in half lengthways (no need to peel). Rest the flat part on the board and slice into each half lengthways and at an angle to make 2cm thick wedges. Toss the wedges in 1 tbsp **olive oil** and ½ tsp **salt**. Lay them flat on a baking tray and roast on the top shelf for around 25–30 mins, or until a little crispy at the edges.

**2** Cut the **tomato** into ½cm slices. Peel and finely chop the **garlic**. Sprinkle a bit of **salt** (less than ¼ tsp) on the **garlic**. Place the flat of your knife on top and drag firmly across the **garlic**. Keep doing this until the **garlic** becomes a paste.

**3** Mix together the **Cajun/Mexican spice** with 2 tbsp **olive oil**. Cut the **halloumi** widthways into 1cm thick slices and pat dry with paper towel. Rub your **Cajun/Mexican** infused oil over the **halloumi**.

**4** Mix the **soured cream** with a tiny bit of your **garlic** paste and a few grinds of **black pepper**. Give it a taste and add more **garlic** paste (if you need to) and **salt** until it tastes just right.

**5** When your **sweet potatoes** are 5 mins away from being cooked, heat a non-stick frying pan over a medium–high heat. Once the pan is hot, gently lay in your **halloumi** and cook for 2 mins on each side, turning only once.

**6** Cut the **buns** in half and put them in your oven for 2 mins (no more) to crisp them up. Meanwhile very, very finely slice (i.e. 'shred') the **baby gem lettuce** widthways. Serve your **halloumi** inside your **buns** with your **lettuce**, **tomato** slices, a dollop of **garlic sauce** and your **sweet potato wedges** on the side (and the rest of the **garlic sauce** for dipping).

# MUSHROOM GNOCCHI

## – WITH A NEW TWIST –

For years I thought the best way to cook gnocchi was by boiling it, but then Renee came along. Renee is a bit of a legend. She was in charge of recipe planning as we started to expand, which meant she regularly bossed me about when I was cooking (I appreciated the discipline really). She also suggested that I fry my gnocchi instead of boiling it, taking the flavour and texture to the next level and one that we still like to recommend today.

**READY IN 35 MINS**

**SERVES** (2)

## Ingredients

- olive oil
- 350g gnocchi
- 1 echalion shallot (the long one), ¼cm dice
- 1 garlic clove, finely chopped
- 3 tbsp fresh flat leaf parsley, roughly chopped
- 150g chestnut mushrooms, quartered
- 20g hard Italian cheese (i.e. veggie Parmesan), grated
- 320g broccoli, bite-sized florets
- 200ml crème fraîche
- salt and black pepper

## Here's how...

**1** Preheat your oven to 100°C/Gas Mark ¼ (just to keep the **gnocchi** warm later).

**2** Heat 2 tbsp **olive oil** in a frying pan over a medium–high heat. Once hot, add the **gnocchi**. Fry until crispy around the edges (about 8 mins) then transfer to a baking tray. Cook the **gnocchi** in batches if your frying pan is not big enough to cook all the **gnocchi** in a single layer (you want it brown and crispy). Pop the baking tray with your **gnocchi** into your oven to keep warm. Keep the pan for making your sauce.

**3** Meanwhile, prep the **shallot**, **garlic** and **parsley**. Cut the **mushrooms** into quarters and grate the **hard Italian cheese**. Cut the **broccoli** into bite-sized florets (like small trees). Bring a large pot of water to the boil with 1 tsp **salt**. Cook the **broccoli** in the boiling water for 3 mins, then remove, drain and keep to the side.

**4** Heat 1 tbsp **olive oil** in your (now empty) frying pan over a high heat. Add the **shallot** and cook for 4 mins or until soft. Add another 1 tbsp **olive oil** if the pan is quite dry, together with the **mushrooms** and cook for 5 mins, until they are nice and soft. Add the **garlic** and cook for 1 min more.

**5** Add 100ml water and a few grinds of **black pepper** to the pan. Allow to simmer over a medium heat for around 8 mins until the water has almost completely gone.

**6** Stir the **crème fraîche** into your **mushroom** mixture. Add your **gnocchi**, **broccoli**, half the **parsley** and **cheese** and give it all a good stir, making sure everything is nicely warmed through. Taste for seasoning and add more **salt** and **black pepper** if necessary. Divide your **gnocchi** between your bowls and top with the remaining grated **cheese** and **parsley**.

# HOMEMADE ROCKET PESTO ORZOTTO
## – WITH CHARRED COURGETTES & TOMATO SALAD –

🕐 **READY IN 40 MINS**　　　　**SERVES** ②

Step aside spaghetti! Peace out penne! Our chef Mimi decided to switch up the usual options when she knocked together this recipe. Orzo is the best pasta shape you've (possibly) never had. They say that necessity is the mother of all invention and when Mimi couldn't find any basil in the kitchen she decided to make this pesto using rocket instead. It's a great twist on a classic and perfect for using up any leftover leaves from last night's salad too.

*Ingredients*

- 2 echalion shallots (the long ones), ½cm dice
- 2 garlic cloves, finely chopped
- 1 courgette, 1cm dice
- 2 vine tomatoes, 1cm dice
- 40g fresh basil leaves, finely chopped
- 60g rocket leaves, finely chopped
- 40g pine nuts
- 3 tbsp hard Italian cheese (i.e. veggie Parmesan), grated
- olive oil
- ½ lemon
- 200g orzo pasta
- 1 vegetable stock pot
- salt and black pepper

*Here's how...*

**1** Prep the shallots, garlic, courgette, tomatoes, basil and rocket.
**Tip: Don't worry, there may be a lot of prep, but it's all plain sailing from here.**

**2** Now for the pesto. Put a frying pan over a medium heat (no oil) and add the **pine nuts**. Dry fry them for 1 min, until they turn golden. Watch them like a hawk or they will burn. Once golden, tip the **pine nuts** onto your chopping board and chop them as finely as you can.

**3** Put your finely chopped **basil**, **rocket** and **pine nuts** in a bowl. Sprinkle in the **hard Italian cheese**, ¼ tsp **salt**, a few good grinds of **black pepper** and pour in 6 tbsp **olive oil**. Add a quarter of your **garlic** and mix everything together thoroughly. If you have a food processor you can use it here, but we like the old fashioned way.

**4** Squeeze the **lemon juice** into another larger bowl and pour in 1 tbsp **olive oil**. Add your **tomato** and a quarter of your chopped **shallot**. Mix everything together and leave to the side.

**5** Put your remaining chopped **shallot** in a saucepan with 1 tbsp **olive oil** over a medium heat and cook for 3–4 mins, before adding your remaining **garlic** and cooking for 1 min more. Add the **orzo pasta** and stir it around until it is nicely coated in the garlicky oil, then pour in 400ml water with the **vegetable stock pot** and stir to dissolve the **stock pot**.

**6** Bring to a gentle boil, then turn the heat down slightly and simmer away for 10 mins or until the liquid has been absorbed and the **pasta** is 'al dente' (cooked through but with a tiny bit of firmness left in the middle). Stir from time to time to ensure it doesn't stick to the bottom of the pan. If all the liquid has been absorbed and the **pasta** is not quite cooked, just add 2 tbsp water and keep cooking.

**7** While your **pasta** is cooking, put the pan you used for your **pine nuts** back over a medium heat without any oil. Once the pan is hot, add your **courgette** and cook for 7–8 mins until charred, turning occasionally. Once charred, remove the pan from the heat.

**8** Once your **pasta** is cooked, stir through three-quarters of your **pesto** along with your charred **courgette**. Serve on plates with your remaining **rocket**, the **tomato salad** and a spoonful of leftover **pesto** on top.

### Hello
## AL DENTE

'Al dente' literally translates as 'to the tooth'. It means there should be a tiny bit of firmness left in the middle of the pasta.

# A LIFE-CHANGING MINT & PEA RISOTTO
## – WITH ASPARAGUS & GOATS' CHEESE –

**READY IN 45 MINS**  |  **SERVES** (2)

One of the recipe-making rules we've always stuck to is never using any equipment in our kitchen that wouldn't appear in the most basic kitchen set-up. No fancy food processors or sous vide machines for us. It's all about making dinnertime simple. That said … if you happen to have a blender at home we'd recommend whizzing the peas in this recipe with a few tablespoons of the stock then pouring into the mixture at the end. It'll turn your whole risotto a vibrant green colour.

### Ingredients

- 1 onion, ½cm dice
- 2 garlic cloves, finely chopped
- 2 tbsp fresh mint leaves, roughly chopped
- 230g asparagus spears, halved
- 1 vegetable stock pot
- 2 tbsp butter
- olive oil
- 175g Arborio rice
- 60ml white wine or 2 tbsp white wine vinegar (optional)
- 100g frozen peas
- 100g mild, rindless goats' cheese
- 2 tbsp hard Italian cheese (i.e. veggie Parmesan), grated
- salt and black pepper

### Here's how...

**1** Prep your **onion, garlic** and **mint**. Hold each **asparagus spear** at both ends and bend gently until it snaps. The little piece is the woody end that can be thrown away. Chop the remaining pieces in half.

**2** Put the **stock pot** into a pan with 900ml water and bring this to a boil. Drop your **asparagus** into the water and boil it for 1 min before removing it from the pan with a slotted spoon. Rinse the **asparagus** under cold water to stop it cooking and going soft. Now turn the **stock** to the lowest heat possible to keep it warm (we'll add this into the **risotto** bit by bit later on).

**3** Heat 1 tbsp **butter** and 1 tsp **olive oil** in a non-stick frying pan over a medium–low heat. Cook the **onion**, with ¼ tsp salt, gently for 5 mins, then add the **garlic** for 1 min, being careful not to brown it off. Next add the **rice** for a few mins and coat it in the oil.

**4** When the **rice** has a little translucency around the edges and the **onion** has softened, add the **wine** or **white wine vinegar**, if using, and bubble away for around 30 seconds. If not, just skip to the next step.

**5** Add a ladleful of your **stock** into the **rice**. Stir it gently with a wooden spoon. When the **stock** has almost gone, add another ladleful. Repeat this process until about one ladleful remains (which should take around 25 mins).

**6** If you've got a blender you can now whizz together the **peas** and half a ladle of **stock** until you have a thick **pea sauce** (i.e. a 'purée'). Pour it into the **risotto** and stir until everything turns a beautiful green (if you don't have a blender don't worry, just add the whole **peas** in step 7).

**7** Taste the **rice** (be careful, it's hot). It should be soft yet with a slight firmness in the centre (if not, add half to one ladle of water and cook a little longer). At this point turn the heat to low and stir in the **goats' cheese**, **frozen peas** (if you didn't blend them before) and **mint**. Finely chop all but four **asparagus spears** and stir these through too.

**8** Stir through half the **Italian cheese** with 1 tbsp **butter** and remove from the heat. Add up to 1 tsp **salt** (taste as you go to get it just right) and a few grinds of **black pepper**. Serve into bowls, cut the **asparagus spears** in half lengthways and lay on top with the remaining **cheese**.

# SWEETCORN FRITTERS
## – WITH AVOCADO, TOMATO & FETA –

**READY IN 30 MINS**          **SERVES ② 2**

Fritters can be tricky little critters. The secret is in the binding. Too little and your fritter will become more of a hash, too much and it'll be dense enough to lay building foundations. For this recipe we found the perfect solution and it became the first HelloFresh outing for a new ingredient: gram flour. Derived from chickpeas, it's a great vegan, gluten-free option and it crisps up to a delicious finish.

### Ingredients

- ½ red chilli, finely chopped
- 3 spring onions, ½cm discs
- 3 tbsp fresh coriander, roughly chopped
- 1 lime, zest and juice
- 260g tinned sweetcorn (drained weight of 1 can)
- 100g gram (i.e. chickpea) flour
- 220g cherry tomatoes, halved lengthways
- 1 avocado, 2cm dice
- 100g feta
- 1 tsp honey
- olive oil
- 1 tbsp pumpkin seeds
- 1 tbsp sweet chilli sauce
- salt and black pepper

### Here's how...

**1** Prep the **chilli**, **spring onions** and **coriander**. Zest and juice the **lime**. Drain the **sweetcorn** in a sieve. Add everything to a mixing bowl save for half the **lime juice**.

**2** Put the **gram flour** in the mixing bowl. Season with ½ tsp **salt** and a few grinds of **black pepper**. Give everything a good stir before adding 50ml water. Then stir everything together again. You should have quite a thick, chunky batter. Set aside for a few mins while you make the **salad**.

**3** Cut the **cherry tomatoes** in half lengthways. Slice the **avocado** in half vertically, twist apart and remove the stone. Slip a spoon around the edge of the flesh to pop the **avocado** out of its skin then chop it into 2cm dice.

**4** Put the **tomatoes** and **avocado** in a mixing bowl and crumble over the **feta**, reserving a few pieces. Add the remaining **lime juice**, the **honey** and 2 tbsp **olive oil**. Season with ¼ tsp **salt** and a few grinds of **black pepper**. Toss through the **pumpkin seeds**.

**5** Put 1½ tbsp **olive oil** in a frying pan over a medium–high heat. Once the pan is hot, spoon in separate heaped tablespoons of the **batter** (we made three small fritters per person but you can make bigger or smaller ones as you like). Cook for 4 mins on the first side and don't touch them, they need to get a good side on them to stick together. Turn carefully and cook for 4 mins more. Once ready, remove to a plate covered in paper towel (to soak up any excess oil). If you have any remaining **batter**, repeat the process.

**6** Serve your **salad** on a plate and pile your **fritters** on top. Crumble the last bits of **feta** over the top and add some **sweet chilli sauce** on the side.

# RAINBOW PEPPER FAJITAS

## – WITH HOMEMADE REFRIED BEANS & CITRUS SOURED CREAM –

🌓 **READY IN 35 MINS**          **SERVES** ②

I remember the moment I first got excited about cooking. I learned how to make a béchamel sauce and thought, 'Blimey, I just made something we'd normally buy ready-made in a jar.' I was hooked. That feeling of making something from scratch was like magic to me. We've been hoping to share that magic since we started HelloFresh, and homemade refried beans have always been a customer favourite.

### *Ingredients*

- 1 red pepper, 1cm slices
- 1 green pepper, 1cm slices
- 1 yellow pepper, 1cm slices
- 1 red onion, 1cm dice
- 3 tbsp fresh coriander, roughly chopped
- 1 tin mixed beans, drained and rinsed
- olive oil
- 1 tsp ground cumin
- ¼ tsp chilli flakes
- 1 tbsp tomato purée
- 1 lime, zest and juice
- 150ml soured cream
- 4 wholemeal tortillas
- 40g rocket leaves
- salt and black pepper

## *Here's how...*

**1** Preheat your oven to 190°C/Gas Mark 5. Prep the **peppers, red onion** and **coriander**. Drain and rinse the **mixed beans** in a colander.

**2** Spread the **peppers** out on a baking tray. Drizzle over 1 tbsp **olive oil** and season with ¼ tsp **salt** and a good grind of **black pepper**. Roast on the top shelf of your oven until soft and a little crispy round the edges, 20–25 mins. If the **peppers** are done before you're finished with everything else, just take them out of your oven, then pop them back in to warm through for a couple of mins before serving.

**3** Heat 1 tbsp **olive oil** in a frying pan over a medium heat and add the **onion**. Cook for 5–7 mins, until soft. Add the **mixed beans, cumin, chilli flakes** (start with a bit, then add more to your taste), **tomato purée** and 100ml water. Season with ¼ tsp **salt** and a few grinds of **black pepper**. Cook over a medium–low heat with the lid on for 15 mins, until the **beans** start to break down.

**4** Zest the whole **lime** and stir half the **zest** into the **soured cream**. Cut the **lime** in half and squeeze 1 tsp of the **juice** in, then taste and add more if you like. Add ¼ tsp **salt** and a few grinds of **black pepper**. Stir it all together, check that you like the level of seasoning and add more if you like. Keep to one side.

**5** To make the **refried beans**, remove half the **bean mixture** to a bowl. Mash the remaining **beans** in the pan into a paste with a potato masher or the back of a fork. Return the reserved **beans** to the pan along with half the **coriander**. Taste and add a little more **salt** if necessary.

**6** Put the **tortillas** in your oven to warm for 2 mins (reheat the **peppers** at this stage too, if necessary). Toss the **rocket** in a 1 tsp of leftover **lime** juice, 1 tsp **olive oil**, a bit of **salt** (less than ¼ tsp) and a grinding of **black pepper**. Serve the **peppers, refried beans, citrus soured cream, rocket** and remaining **coriander** in separate bowls so everyone can dive in and create their own **fajitas**.

# SPRINGTIME PESTO & ASPARAGUS TART
## – WITH ROCKET & TOASTED PINE NUTS –

**READY IN 30 MINS**          **SERVES** (2)

It's not fair to choose favourites. Nevertheless, this little number gets to sit in the front seat of the car every time. Now, granted, you could make your own pastry, but there are a lot of great pre-made versions out there that'll save you a sackload of time, which can be better invested elsewhere.*

*A colour-coded sock drawer is a thing of beauty.

### Ingredients

- 150g asparagus spears, halved lengthways
- 50ml crème fraîche
- 1½ tbsp ready-made basil pesto
- 3 tbsp hard Italian cheese (i.e. veggie Parmesan), grated
- 1 sheet (320g) all-butter puff pastry
- 2 tbsp pine nuts
- 1 tbsp milk
- 40g rocket
- olive oil
- salt and black pepper

### Here's how...

**1** Preheat your oven to 200°C/Gas Mark 6 and boil a large pan of water. Hold each **asparagus spear** at both ends and bend gently until it snaps. The little piece is the woody end that can be thrown away. Chop the remaining pieces in half lengthways and boil for 1 min. Drain then run under cold water for 15 seconds and pat dry

**2** Mix the **crème fraîche** with the **pesto** and half the grated **cheese**.

**3** Unroll the **pastry** onto a lightly greased baking tray and use a knife to lightly mark a border around it, 1cm from the edge.

**4** Spread the **crème fraîche mixture** inside the border. Place the **asparagus** over the **mixture**.

**5** Scatter the **pine nuts** on top, brush the pastry border with **milk** and bake for 15–20 mins until the **pastry** has risen and is nice and golden.

**6** Mix your **rocket** with 2 tsp of your best-quality **olive oil**, a bit of **salt** (less than ¼ tsp) and a few grinds of **black pepper**.

**7** Scatter the **rocket** and remaining **cheese** over the cooked **tart** and serve it straight away. **Tip:** We like serving one large tart to cut at the table but you can make mini ones of you like.

# – SPICED MOROCCAN –
# LENTIL & CHICKPEA SOUP

'Bringing the world to your kitchen' may sound like something from an ad campaign, but as HelloFresh developed we knew we had a chance to take people's tastebuds on a trip. The tricky thing with trying exotic new recipes is the risk that they're not going to turn out that well after you've invested in all those spices. Fear not – this recipe is a customer favourite that you'll return to time and time again. Best eaten with a North African playlist for maximum effect.

🕐 **READY IN 40 MINS**

**SERVES** ②

## Ingredients

- 1 red onion,
  ½cm half moons
- 1 tin chickpeas,
  drained and rinsed
- 2 tbsp fresh coriander
  leaves, roughly chopped
- 1 tbsp fresh coriander
  stalks, roughly chopped
- olive oil
- 1 tsp ground cumin
- 1½ tsp ras-el-hanout
- 1 tsp smoked paprika
- 1 tin chopped tomatoes
- 1 tbsp tomato purée
- 1 vegetable stock pot
- 50g red lentils, rinsed
- ½ tsp Tabasco sauce
  (optional)
- 1 ciabatta
- 100g Greek yoghurt
- salt and black pepper

## Here's how...

**1** Prep the **onion**. Drain and rinse the **chickpeas** in a colander. Separate the **coriander leaves** from the **stalks** and roughly chop both (keep separate).

**2** Heat 1½ tbsp **olive oil** in a large saucepan over a medium heat and add the **cumin**, **ras-el-hanout** and **smoked paprika**. After 1 min, add your **onion** and cook until soft, around 5 mins. Add the **coriander stalks** and cook for 1 min more. Add ½ tsp **salt**.

**3** Add the **chopped tomatoes**, **tomato purée** and 500ml water together with the **vegetable stock pot**. Stir to dissolve and bring the mixture to a gentle boil.

**4** Rinse the **red lentils** thoroughly under running water for 1 min, then add to your **soup** along with the **chickpeas**. Simmer for 15 mins. Next up, add half the **coriander leaves** and cook for 10 more mins or until the **lentils** are soft. Once your **soup** has thickened, taste for seasoning and add **salt** if necessary. **Tip: I add a bit of Tabasco to spice things up.**

**5** Meanwhile, preheat your grill to its highest setting. Cut the **ciabatta** in half lengthways and toast on each side under your grill. Drizzle over a little **olive oil** and a small amount of **salt** (adjust depending on the size of the pieces).

**6** Serve your **soup** in bowls with your remaining **coriander** sprinkled on top. Dollop on some **Greek yoghurt** and serve with your toasted **ciabatta** on the side.

# SMOKEY RATATOUILLE
## – WITH GARLIC CIABATTA –

**READY IN 35 MINS**        **SERVES** ②

This one's an oldie but a goodie, back from when HelloFresh was knee-high to a grasshopper. Regular paprika is made by drying peppers in the sun then grinding them to a powder. For the smoked variety, the peppers are dried in smoke sheds using wood such as oak to impart a distinctive flavour. It's a great store cupboard addition and brings a whole new dimension to your cooking. For this recipe, we balanced it against fresh, mild goats' cheese.

## *Ingredients*

- 1 yellow pepper, 1cm lengthways strips
- 1 red pepper, 1cm lengthways strips
- 2 courgettes, 1cm dice
- 2 garlic cloves, one finely chopped, one halved
- 1 aubergine, 2cm dice
- olive oil
- 2 tbsp pine nuts
- ¾ tsp smoked paprika
- 1 tin chopped tomatoes
- ¼ tsp sugar
- 1 ciabatta
- 3 tbsp fresh basil leaves, roughly chopped
- 75g rindless goats' cheese
- 50g ready-made green pesto
- salt and black pepper

## *Here's how...*

**1** Preheat your oven to 220°C/Gas Mark 7. Prep the **peppers, courgettes** and **garlic**. Trim the top and bottom off the **aubergine** and discard. Cut the **aubergine** in half lengthways, then slice each half lengthways into 2cm thick slices. Now line up the slices and chop widthways into 2cm dice.

**2** Put the **peppers, courgette** and **aubergine** on a large baking tray, then drizzle over 1½ tbsp **olive oil**. Season with ½ tsp **salt** and a few grinds of **black pepper**. Toss to coat, then pop on the top shelf of your oven. Roast until softened and slightly crisp at the edges, about 20–25 mins.

**3** In a dry frying pan, toast your **pine nuts** over a medium–high heat until golden. Remove from the pan and set aside

**4** In the same pan (no need to wash up), heat 1 tbsp **olive oil** over a medium heat. Fry the **garlic** and the **paprika** for 1 min. Add the **chopped tomatoes** and **sugar**. Refill the tin a quarter of the way with water and swirl around to grab all of the tomatoey goodness and add to the pan. Season with ¼ tsp **salt** and a few grinds of **black pepper**. Lower the heat and simmer until you have a thick **tomato sauce**, about 10–15 mins, stirring occasionally.

**5** Cut the **ciabatta** in half lengthways (as if you were making a sandwich). Put them in the oven for 2 mins until they are toasted a nice golden brown. Cut the remaining **garlic clove** in half and rub this across the cut side of the **ciabatta**. Very lightly coat with a little **olive oil** and season with a bit of **salt** and **black pepper** (adjust the amount depending on the size of each piece).

**6** Tear the **basil leaves** and add two-thirds to the **tomato sauce** along with the **roasted veggies**. Stir to combine. If your **pesto** is quite thick, add a little **olive oil** to let it down to a drizzling consistency. Serve the **smokey ratatouille** in a bowl and scatter over the remaining **basil leaves** and the **pine nuts**. Crumble on the **goats' cheese**, drizzle the **green pesto** over the top and serve with the **garlic bread** on the side.

# QUICKDRAW QUESADILLAS
## – WITH TOMATO & CORN SALSA –

Ahhh, the magic of photography. When we first started HelloFresh our photography set-up was a little rudimentary to say the least. I remember us taking the original photo for this recipe in the little alleyway behind my house and trying to make it look like a Mexican restaurant. Thankfully things have come on a long way since then. Arriba!

**READY IN 35 MINS**

**SERVES** ②

## Ingredients

- 1 red onion, ½cm dice
- 1 garlic clove, finely chopped
- 3 tbsp fresh coriander, roughly chopped
- 100g Cheddar, grated
- 2 corn on the cobs
- olive oil
- 1 tbsp Mexican spice mix
- 1 tsp smoked paprika
- 1 tin black beans, drained and rinsed
- 4 soft large flour tortillas
- 2 vine tomatoes, 1cm dice
- 1 baby gem lettuce, thinly shredded
- 1 lime, zest and juice
- 150ml soured cream
- salt and black pepper

## Here's how...

**1** Prep the **onion** and **garlic**. Separate the **coriander leaves** from the **stalks**, roughly chop both but keep them separate. Grate the **Cheddar**. Place the **corn on the cob** upright on a chopping board and cut straight down one side. Continue cutting around the whole **cob** until all the **corn** is removed.

**2** Put 1 tbsp **olive oil** in a frying pan over a medium heat. Add three-quarters of the **red onion** and cook until soft, about 5 mins. Add the **garlic** and **coriander stalks** and cook for 1 min. Add the **Mexican spice** and **smoked paprika** and cook until you can smell it, 1 min. Taste and gradually season with **salt** and **black pepper**. Remove from the heat and transfer to a mixing bowl.

**3** Drain and rinse the **black beans** in a colander and add to the bowl. Mix everything together and roughly mash with a potato masher or the back of a fork. Stir in half the **coriander leaves**, the **corn** kernels and the **Cheddar**. Taste to check the seasoning and add more **salt** and **black pepper** if needed.

**4** To make the **quesadillas**, lay the **tortillas** flat and divide the filling evenly between them. Spread it out over half of each **tortilla** then fold the other half over to make semicircular 'sandwiches'. Set aside.

**5** Prep the **tomatoes** and 'shred' (i.e. very thinly slice widthways) the **baby gem lettuce**, then combine with the remaining **red onion** and **coriander leaves** in a small bowl. Zest and juice the **lime**. Add half the **lime juice**, 2 tbsp **olive oil** and season with ¼ tsp **salt** and a few grinds of **black pepper**. Put the **soured cream** in another small bowl and mix in the remaining **lime juice**. Season with ½ tsp **salt** and a few grinds of **black pepper** and add **lime zest** to taste.

**6** Wash and dry your frying pan and put it back over a medium heat with a drizzle of **oil**. Fry two of your folded **quesadillas** at a time until golden brown, about 4 mins per side. Serve with the **salsa** and **soured cream** and let everyone help themselves.

## Hello
# BREAKFAST

If you have any spare filling then save it for the morning and fry it like a hash brown. Serve with a fried egg on top.

# CAULIFLOWER & LENTIL DAL

Since HelloFresh started we've been sending out a questionnaire to our customers for every recipe they receive. And it's helped us to get better. We develop each recipe based on exactly what everyone tells us they like and, as a result, the scores go up and up. This dal was borne of that exact process. After sending it out the first time we tweaked it based on the feedback and now it's one of the most popular dishes in our archive.

🕐 **READY IN 40 MINS**

**SERVES** ②

## Ingredients

- 1 **red onion**, ½cm dice
- 1 **garlic clove**, finely chopped
- 3 tbsp **fresh coriander**, roughly chopped
- 500g **cauliflower**, bite-sized florets
- 150g **green beans**, trimmed and chopped into thirds
- **olive oil**
- 1 tbsp **curry powder**
- 1 tbsp **tomato purée**
- 1 tin **chopped tomatoes**
- ¼ tsp **sugar**
- 100g **red lentils**
- 1 **vegetable stock pot**
- 100g **Greek yoghurt**
- **salt and black pepper**

## Here's how...

**1** Prep the **red onion**, **garlic** and **coriander**, and separate the **cauliflower** into bite-sized florets. Trim the ends from the **green beans** and discard. Then chop the **green beans** into three pieces.

**2** Heat 1½ tbsp **olive oil** in a large pot over a medium–low heat. Add your **onion** and slowly cook for 5 mins, turning the heat down if it starts to brown. Add your **garlic** and cook for 1 more min. Season with ¼ tsp **salt** and a few grinds of **black pepper**. Once your **onions** are soft, add the **curry powder** and stir for 1 min.

**3** Stir in the **tomato purée** for 1 min and then add the **chopped tomatoes**. Add another ¼ tsp **salt** and the **sugar**. Add the **red lentils**, 200ml water and the **vegetable stock pot** and stir to dissolve. Bring to a gentle simmer, put a lid on and leave for 5 mins.

**4** Remove the lid and add your **cauliflower**. Simmer for around 15 mins or until tender. Keep testing in the last few mins for 'doneness'. We like ours with a bit of crunch left.

**5** When your **cauliflower** is halfway through cooking, add your **green beans** and cook for 6–7 more mins. If you notice the **dal** drying out a little just add a bit more water to get a looser consistency.

**6** Stir through most of your **coriander** and some of the **yoghurt**, taste for seasoning, then add more **salt** and **black pepper** to lift the flavours to their max if you think it needs it. Serve with the remaining **coriander** and a nice big dollop of **yoghurt**.

# ONE-POT VEGETARIAN CHILLI
## – WITH QUINOA –

**READY IN 30 MINS**  **SERVES** (2)

Say hello to our 'one-pot wonder'. We all know that feeling of getting home late and eyeing up that tin of baked beans in the cupboard. We created recipes like this for those occasions. Maximum taste with minimal fuss and minimal washing up.

## *Ingredients*

- 1 green pepper, ½cm dice
- 1 carrot, ½cm dice
- 3 tbsp fresh coriander, roughly chopped
- 2 garlic cloves, finely chopped
- ½ red onion, finely chopped
- 1 tin kidney beans, drained and rinsed
- olive oil
- 2 tbsp tomato purée
- 1 tbsp ground cumin
- ¾ tsp mild chilli powder
- 1 vegetable stock pot
- 150g quinoa
- 1 tin chopped tomatoes
- 1 lime, zest and juice
- 150ml soured cream
- salt and black pepper

## *Here's how...*

**1** Prep the **pepper**, **carrot**, **coriander**, **garlic** and **onion**. Drain and rinse the **kidney beans** in a colander.

**2** Heat 1 tbsp **olive oil** in a large saucepan over a medium heat. Add the **carrot** and **onion** and gently fry for 5 mins. Now add the **garlic** and **green pepper** for 2 mins before adding the **tomato purée**, **cumin** and **chilli powder** (go easy if you don't like it too spicy). Stir to coat and fry for another 30 seconds.

**3** Add 300ml water to the pan along with the **vegetable stock pot**. Stir to dissolve the **stock pot**, then add the **quinoa**, **kidney beans** and **chopped tomatoes**. Season with ¼ tsp **salt**, a good grind of **black pepper** and stir everything together.

**4** Bring your **chilli** to the boil and then reduce the heat to medium so that it can gently bubble away. Cook until the **quinoa** is tender with a tiny bit of firmness in the middle, about 15 mins, stirring occasionally. Zest the whole **lime** into the **soured cream**, then squeeze in half its **juice**, together with ¼ tsp **salt** and a good grind of **black pepper**.

**5** Stir three-quarters of the **coriander** into the **chilli**. Remove from the heat and serve the **chilli** in bowls topped with some **soured cream**. Sprinkle over the remaining **coriander** and tuck in, adding more **lime juice** if you like it fresh.

# FRESH START AUBERGINE KORMA

## – WITH HOMEMADE WHOLEMEAL CHAPATIS –

**READY IN 35 MINS**　　　　　**SERVES** ②

Once you've had a taste of the good stuff it's very difficult to go back. Nowhere is this more true than when it comes to bread. In this recipe we want to give you a go at making your own, to see just how delicious (and satisfying) it can be. Rather than go in at the deep end though, we're kicking off with the simplest bread of them all: the humble chapati. Prized in India for its easiness to prepare (and the fact that they're awesome for mopping up sauce).

### *Ingredients*

- 125g wholemeal flour
- flavourless oil, or olive oil
- 300g potato, 1cm dice
- 1 garlic clove, finely chopped
- 3 tbsp fresh coriander, roughly chopped
- 1 aubergine, 2cm dice
- ½ red onion, thin half moons
- 1 tsp ground coriander
- 1 tsp ground cumin
- ¾ tsp ground turmeric
- ¼ tsp mild chilli powder (optional)
- 1 vegetable stock pot
- 125g baby spinach
- 200g Greek yoghurt
- 2 tbsp flaked almonds
- salt and black pepper

### *Here's how...*

**1** Put all but 2 tbsp of the **wholemeal flour** into a bowl with ¼ tsp **salt**. Gradually add 50–75ml water whilst you mix it with your hands. Keep mixing and adding until you have a soft (but not soggy) **dough**.

**2** Sprinkle the remaining **flour** onto your work surface and coat the **dough** in 1 tsp **oil**. Knead the **dough** by pushing it away from you on the work surface. Form it back into a ball and then push it away again to stretch it. Once you've pummelled it for a few mins leave it to rest.

**3** Prep the **potato** (no need to peel), **garlic** and **fresh coriander**. Trim the top and bottom off the **aubergine** and discard. Cut the **aubergine** in half lengthways, then slice each half lengthways into 2cm thick slices. Now line up the slices and chop widthways into 2cm dice.

**4** Heat a frying pan over a medium–high heat. Add 2 tbsp **oil** and the **aubergine** and fry, stirring, until golden and slightly softened, about 6–8 mins. Add 1 tbsp **oil**, the **onion** and **garlic** and cook for 5 mins, or until soft. Add the **ground coriander**, **cumin** and **turmeric** and mix well. Now add the **chilli powder** if you'd like a bit of extra heat. Add the **vegetable stock pot** to the pan with 300ml water and stir until dissolved. Add the **potato**, bring to a gentle simmer, reduce the heat to low, cover with a lid and cook for 10–15 mins. Stir every 5 mins.

**5** Once the **curry** has cooked for 10–15 mins with the lid on, remove the lid and let it bubble until reduced by a third (you don't want it watery). Add the **baby spinach**, stir well to combine everything and simmer until the **spinach** wilts. Remove from the heat and wait 5 mins before stirring through half of the **Greek yoghurt** (too hot and the **yoghurt** will split).

**6** Divide your **dough** into 4 pieces, then roll out each piece as thin as a pancake to form your **chapatis**. **Tip: If you don't have a rolling pin you can use a wine bottle or even a tin can.** Place the **chapatis** in a searing hot, dry frying pan and cook on both sides until you see little light brown spots form.

**7** Mix the remaining **Greek yoghurt** with half of your chopped **coriander**, a bit of **salt** (less than ¼ tsp) and a few grinds of **black pepper** to make a 'raita' (AKA yoghurt sauce). Add 1 tbsp water if it is too thick. Serve your **curry** with the **chapatis** and **raita** on the side and sprinkle over the remaining **coriander** and the **flaked almonds**.

## Hello
## CHAPATI

Seeing the action of pummelling the dough action is really helpful. Search 'kneading bread' on YouTube to see how it's done.

# LENTIL & VEGETABLE HOTPOT
## – WITH A CHEESE & POTATO TOPPING –

Don't be put off by the length of the ingredients list as they're all easy to find and the result is a total belter. It would have been easy for us to create a year's worth of recipes in year one and then just repeat them each year after that, but we're all about variety, and the chefs are in the kitchen every day crafting new flavour combinations to keep it exciting. That said, there are a few customer favourites that people demand to see again – and this is one of the more wintery ones.

**READY IN 55 MINS**
(don't worry, most of this is in the oven)

**SERVES** ②

## Ingredients

1 **garlic clove,** finely chopped

1 **onion,** ½cm dice

1 **carrot,** ½cm dice

1 **red pepper,** 1cm dice

150g **chestnut mushrooms,** quartered

1 tin cooked **Puy lentils,** drained and rinsed

2 tbsp fresh **flat leaf parsley,** finely chopped

450g **potato,** ½cm discs

**olive oil**

1½ tsp **Provençal herbs**

1 **vegetable stock pot**

1 tbsp **tomato purée**

1 tbsp **soy sauce**

2 tsp **English mustard**

125g **baby spinach**

2 tbsp **butter**

30g **Cheddar,** grated

**salt** and **black pepper**

## Here's how...

**1** Preheat your oven to 200°C/Gas Mark 6. Prep the **garlic, onion, carrot** and **pepper.** Cut the **chestnut mushrooms** into quarters and drain and rinse the **lentils** in a sieve. Roughly chop the **parsley** (stalks and all). Cut the **potato** (no need to peel) into ½cm thick discs.

**2** Heat 1½ tbsp **olive oil** in a large saucepan over a medium heat. Cook the **onion** until slightly soft, 4–5 mins. Add the **carrot, pepper** and **mushrooms,** along with ¼ tsp **salt** and a few grinds of **black pepper.** Cook until they are also soft, 5 mins. Add the **garlic.** Cook for 1 min more.

**3** Next, add the **lentils** and **Provençal herbs** to the pan and stir well. Pour in 200ml water along with the **vegetable stock pot.** Add the **tomato purée, soy sauce, mustard, baby spinach** and half the **parsley.** It might look like a lot of **spinach** initially but it will wilt down. Stir together then cover with a lid. Simmer for 3–4 mins.

**4** Transfer the **lentil mixture** from the pan into an ovenproof dish. Layer the **potato discs** over the top: don't overlap them too much or they won't all cook at the same rate. Dot the top with **butter** and season with a few grinds of **black pepper,** then put the **hotpot** on the top shelf of your oven. Bake for 20–25 mins. The **potato** will sink slightly into the **lentil mixture** as it cooks, this is perfectly fine.

**5** While your **hotpot** is in your oven, grate the **Cheddar.** Once the 25 mins baking time is up, remove the **hotpot** from the oven and scatter over the **Cheddar.** Turn the grill to high and place the **hotpot** underneath until the **Cheddar** has melted, about 5 mins.

**6** Serve as much as you can handle in a large bowl and garnish with the remaining **parsley.**

# LEEK & POTATO GRATIN
## – WITH GOATS' CHEESE & SPINACH –

The less experienced home chefs out there may be asking 'grat what'? Let our chef André demystify it for you: 'The French terms might sound a bit fancy but the reality is really simple. Gratin originated in French cuisine and is a culinary technique in which an ingredient is topped with a crispy, golden topping. In this recipe we have used our HelloFresh favourite panko breadcrumbs and creamy goats' cheese to give this dish an indulgent, crunchy top.'

**READY IN 40 MINS**

**SERVES** ②

## Ingredients

450g red potato, 2cm dice

2 leeks, 1cm half moons

olive oil

2 tbsp fresh tarragon leaves, roughly chopped

125g rindless mild goats' cheese

3 tbsp hard Italian cheese (i.e. veggie Parmesan), grated

5 tbsp panko breadcrumbs

125g baby spinach

200ml crème fraîche

1 vegetable stock pot

40g rocket leaves

salt and black pepper

## Here's how...

**1** Boil a large pot of water. Prep the **potato** (no need to peel), remove the root and dark green part from the **leeks** and prep the remainder. Add the **potato** to the boiling water with ½ tsp **salt** and simmer for 15–20 mins. The **potato** is cooked when you can easily slip a knife through. Once cooked, drain your **potato** in a colander and keep to one side.

**2** Heat 1½ tbsp **olive oil** in a wide-bottomed saucepan over a medium heat. Add your **leeks** and cook for 5–6 mins, stirring frequently. You want the **leeks** to soften and not brown off so turn the heat lower if you need to. Meanwhile, pull the **tarragon leaves** from the stalks and roughly chop them (discard the stalks).

**3** Add 50ml water to the **leeks**, bring to the boil, then reduce the heat to medium and cook for 7 mins whilst continually stirring. You want the **leeks** to be completely soft.

**4** Cut the **goats' cheese** into six even slices. Keep to one side. Mix the **hard Italian cheese** with the **panko breadcrumbs** in a bowl. Season with ¼ tsp **salt**, a few grinds of **black pepper** and 2 tbsp **olive oil**. Keep to one side. Preheat your grill to medium–high.

**5** Add the **baby spinach** to your **leek** mixture and cook for a further 2 mins until wilted. Your **potato** should be cooked by now, so add it to the pan as well. Sprinkle in the **tarragon leaves** and then stir in the **crème fraîche** and **stock pot** and bring the mixture up to a gentle bubble. Add 1 tsp **salt** and a few grinds of **black pepper** and stir to make sure the **stock pot** dissolves.

**6** Spoon your **leek** mixture into an ovenproof dish and sprinkle your **cheesy breadcrumbs** on top. Finish with your **goats' cheese** slices and put under your grill for 3–5 mins. You want your **goats' cheese** to melt and the crumb to brown nicely. Serve with a good handful of **rocket** alongside.

## Hello
## LEEKS

Leeks are so versatile. Try
lightly coating them in olive oil,
salt and black pepper and
roasting them to make a
delicious side dish.

# TANDOORI-SPICED AUBERGINE
## – WITH TOMATO & CORIANDER RICE & NIGELLA YOGHURT –

**READY IN 35 MINS**     **SERVES** (2)

When our chef, André, has vegetarian friends over for dinner this has become his go-to dish. The flavour would make you think a lot more hard work goes into it, but you can have it on the table in no time at all. Be warned: this dish will get you a reputation as an ace vegetarian cook, so expect to be hosting a lot more dinners after you've made it.

### Ingredients

- 1 aubergine, quartered lengthways
- 1 tbsp tandoori spice mix
- olive oil
- 1 red onion, ½cm dice
- 1 red pepper, 1cm dice
- 2 garlic cloves, crushed or finely chopped
- 1 tbsp fresh ginger, peeled and finely chopped
- ½ tsp ground turmeric
- 150g basmati rice
- 1 vegetable stock pot
- 3 spring onions, ½cm discs
- 3 tbsp fresh coriander, roughly chopped
- 200g cherry tomatoes, quartered
- ½ tsp nigella seeds
- 150g Greek yoghurt
- salt and black pepper

### Here's how...

**1** Preheat your oven to 200°C/Gas Mark 6. Trim off the top and bottom of the **aubergine**. Cut the **aubergine** lengthways into four long wedges. Mix ½ tsp **salt**, the **tandoori spice** (don't use it all if you're not a fan of spice) and 1 tbsp **olive oil** together in a small bowl. Massage this into the **aubergine** and then pop it on a baking tray. Roast on the middle shelf of your oven for 25 mins.

**2** Prep the **onion, red pepper, garlic** and **ginger**.

**3** Heat 1½ tbsp **olive oil** in a large saucepan over a medium heat. Add the **onion** and **pepper** and cook until soft (about 5 mins). Add the **ginger** and half the **garlic**. Cook for 30 seconds more. Stir in the **turmeric** and **basmati rice** and then pour in 300ml water. Bring to the boil and then stir in the **vegetable stock pot**.

**4** Turn the heat to medium, put a lid on the pan and cook for 10 mins. After this, remove from the heat, but don't peek under the lid until 20 mins are up. As the **rice** cooks, prep your **spring onions** and **coriander** (stalks and all). Cut the **cherry tomatoes** into quarters. Put the **spring onions, coriander** and **cherry tomatoes** in a small bowl with the remaining **garlic** and mix together to make a chunky **salsa**. Season with a bit of **salt** (less than ¼ tsp) and keep to one side.

**5** When your **rice** is cooked, add half the **salsa** and gently stir it through the rice. Mix the **nigella seeds** into the **yoghurt**.

**6** Serve your **aubergine** on top of a generous pile of **rice** and finish with some of the remaining **salsa** and a few dollops of **Nigella yoghurt**.

# VEGGIE SHEPHERD'S PIE

🕐 **READY IN 45 MINS**  **SERVES** ②

If we've learned one thing over the years, it's that vegetarian recipes need to be good and hearty. When the nights draw in and the frost starts to settle, a little salad just won't do. This dish of deliciousness was born one chilly autumn to inject a bit of comfort into dinnertime. We recommend making enough for four people and saving some for later in the week, so double the quantities if you like.

## Ingredients

- 500g potato, 2cm dice
- 1 onion, ½cm dice
- 1 carrot, 1cm dice
- 1 stick celery, 1cm dice
- 1 garlic clove, finely chopped
- ½ tbsp fresh rosemary, finely chopped
- 3 tbsp fresh flat leaf parsley, finely chopped
- 150g chestnut mushrooms, quartered
- olive oil
- 60g Cheddar, grated
- 1 tin cooked Puy lentils, drained and rinsed
- 1½ tsp ground coriander
- 200g tomato passata
- 1 vegetable stock pot
- 1 tbsp Worcestershire sauce
- 2 tbsp butter
- salt and black pepper

## Here's how...

**1** Put a pan of water with 1 tsp **salt** over a high heat. Prep the **potato** (no need to peel) and pop them into your pan of water. Bring to the boil, then lower the heat to medium and cook for 15–20 mins. The **potatoes** are cooked when you can easily slip a knife through them.

**2** Prep the **onion, carrot, celery, garlic, rosemary** and **parsley**. Cut the **mushrooms** into quarters.

**3** Heat 1½ tbsp **olive oil** in a saucepan over a medium heat. When hot, add the **onion, carrot, celery** and **mushrooms**. Season with ½ tsp **salt** and a few grinds of **black pepper**. Cook until soft, 5–7 mins, with the lid on, stirring occasionally. Whilst the veggies cook, finish your last few prep jobs: grate the **Cheddar**, then drain and rinse the **lentils** in a sieve.

**4** Add the **garlic, ground coriander** and **rosemary** to the veggies and cook for 1 min more. Pour in the **tomato passata** and 110ml water. Stir in the **vegetable stock pot** until it's dissolved. Lower the heat so the sauce is bubbling away and then add half the **Worcestershire sauce**. Cook with the lid off until the **carrots** are tender and the sauce has reduced by half, 15 mins.

**5** When the **potato** is cooked, drain in a colander and then return to the pan off the heat. Mash the **potato** with a potato masher or the back of a fork. Add the **butter**, mix well and then season with ½ tsp **salt** and a few grinds of **black pepper**. Keep to one side. Preheat your grill to its highest setting.

**6** Test a **carrot** in the sauce to check they're cooked (continue cooking for 5 mins if not) and then add the **lentils**. Stir in the **parsley** and add more **salt** and **black pepper** if needed. Spoon the **sauce** into an ovenproof baking dish and then top with the **mash**. Smooth the **mash** over with a spoon then sprinkle on the **cheese** and remaining **Worcestershire sauce**. Put under the grill for 3 mins until the **cheese** is golden and bubbling, then serve.

# CAULIFLOWER & LENTIL PANANG CURRY

When this recipe first went on our menu back in 2013 we felt like we were pretty 'down with the kids'. Cauliflower was just beginning to free itself from the shackles of congealed cheese and was popping up in all sorts of exciting restaurants across London. When the growing team gave it a try, it got an all-round thumbs up, but they also politely explained that using the phrase 'down with the kids' probably didn't help our street cred. We renamed it accordingly.

**READY IN 30 MINS**

**SERVES** ②

## *Ingredients*

**175g brown rice**

**1 tin cooked green lentils,** drained and rinsed

**1 onion,** ½cm dice

**1 tbsp fresh ginger,** peeled and finely chopped

**1 garlic clove,** finely chopped

**150g green beans,** trimmed and chopped into thirds

**olive oil**

**1 tbsp panang curry paste** (or **red curry paste**)

**400ml coconut milk**

**1 vegetable stock pot**

**150g cauliflower,** bite-sized florets

**3 tbsp fresh coriander,** roughly chopped

**1 lime,** cut into wedges (optional)

**salt and black pepper**

## *Here's how...*

**1** Bring a large pot of water to a rapid boil over a high heat. Rinse the **brown rice** under running water for 30 seconds. Add the **rice** with ½ tsp **salt** to the boiling water and cook over a high heat for around 25 mins (topping up the water if you need to).

**2** Drain and thoroughly rinse the **lentils**. Prep the **onion, ginger** and **garlic**. Trim the ends from the **green beans** and discard. Then chop the **green beans** into three pieces.

**3** Heat 1 tbsp **olive oil** in a frying pan over a medium–low heat. Once warm, add your **onion** with ¼ tsp **salt** and a few grinds of **black pepper** and slowly cook for 5 mins.

**4** Add the **ginger, garlic** and **panang curry paste** and cook for 1 min before adding the **coconut milk**. Add the **vegetable stock pot** with 50ml water, stir to dissolve and turn the heat to medium. Allow the sauce to reduce for around 8 mins until it is thicker.

**5** Cut the **cauliflower** into bite-sized florets. Add these and your **green beans** to your **curry sauce** and cook for 5–7 mins, or until the **cauliflower** is cooked.

**6** Lastly chop the **coriander** and stir both this and your **lentils** through your **curry**, before serving it on top of your **brown rice**. If you like, you can cut the **lime** into wedges and serve on the side for people to squeeze over their **curry** at the table.

# MEXICAN BUCKWHEAT BAKE

🕐 **READY IN 40 MINS**                    **SERVES** ②

Some celebrities like to flaunt themselves to the masses, whilst others are more incognito. Trendy quinoa might fall into the former category, whilst buckwheat stays under the radar. However, quiet buckwheat hides a deeply nutritious secret: it's not actually a wheat at all, but a seed related to rhubarb. It's full of goodness and nutty flavour, and though this recipe was the first time I'd ever used it, it became an instant hit. Take a walk on the wild side and discover buckwheat's hidden talent.

## *Ingredients*

- 1 red and 1 yellow pepper, 2cm dice
- olive oil
- 1 vegetable stock pot
- 150g buckwheat
- 1 red onion, ½cm dice
- 1 green chilli, finely chopped
- 1 garlic clove, finely chopped
- 2 tbsp fresh chives, finely chopped or snipped
- 1 tin black beans, drained and rinsed
- ¾ tsp ground cumin
- ¾ tsp paprika
- ½ tsp cayenne pepper
- ¾ tsp ground cinnamon
- 100ml crème fraîche
- 60g Cheddar, grated
- salt and black pepper

## *Here's how...*

**1** Preheat your oven to 220°C/Gas Mark 7. Line a baking tray with baking paper. Prep the **peppers** and place on the lined tray. Drizzle over 1 tbsp **olive oil** and toss together. Roast on the top shelf of your oven until slightly crispy at the edges, 15 mins.

**2** Meanwhile, boil 275ml water in a medium saucepan and stir in the **vegetable stock pot**. Add the **buckwheat**. Bring back to the boil and cover with a lid. Cook over a medium heat for 10 mins. Then remove from the heat and set aside (don't take off the lid). The **buckwheat** is cooked when it's soft but not mushy; it should retain a slight nuttiness.

**3** Prep the **red onion**, **green chilli**, **garlic** and **chives**, then drain and rinse the **black beans** in a colander.

**4** Heat 1 tbsp **olive oil** in a frying pan over a medium heat. Add the **onion** and **chilli** (a bit less if you aren't keen on spice) and cook until softened, 5 mins. Add the **cumin**, **paprika**, **garlic**, **cayenne pepper** and **cinnamon**. Cook for 1 min more. Add the **black beans** and season with ½ tsp **salt** and a few grinds of **black pepper**. Cook for 1 min more, then remove from the heat.

**5** Once the **buckwheat** is done (it should be dry not soggy), fluff it up with a fork to separate the grains. Combine with your **black bean mixture**. Add the **roasted peppers** and stir through half the **crème fraîche**. Taste for seasoning and add more **salt** or **black pepper** if necessary.

**6** Tip the **buckwheat** and **black bean mixture** into an ovenproof dish and grate the **Cheddar** over the top. Place on the top shelf of your oven. Bake until the top is beautifully golden and crisp, about 10 mins. Serve with the remaining **crème fraîche** and a scattering of **chives**.

# VEGETABLE-PACKED TOMATOEY MOUSSAKA
## – WITH CHEAT'S GARLIC BREAD –

If cheating means cutting out all the hard work and just leaving the fun bit, then we're OK with that. Dishes like lasagne and moussaka seem out of reach for a mid-week dinner because of the time they take, but our chef Mimi had other ideas. You'll have this little number on the table so fast that people will want an action replay to check you really cooked it.

**READY IN 35 MINS**

**SERVES** 2

## Ingredients

1 **onion**, ½cm dice

1 **courgette**, ½cm dice

1 **yellow pepper**, 1cm dice

2 tsp **fresh oregano leaves**, finely chopped

2 **garlic cloves**, one finely chopped, one whole

1 **aubergine**, 1cm lengthways slices

50g **red lentils**, rinsed

**olive oil**

1 **cinnamon stick**

2 tbsp **tomato purée**

1 tbsp **Worcestershire sauce**

1 **vegetable stock cube**, crumbled

1 **tin chopped tomatoes**

1 **ciabatta**

100ml **crème fraîche**

40g **hard Italian cheese** (i.e. veggie Parmesan), grated

**salt** and **black pepper**

## Here's how...

**1** Preheat the grill to high. Prep the **onion, courgette, yellow pepper** and **oregano**. Peel and finely chop one of the **garlic** cloves. Trim the top and bottom off the **aubergine** and discard. Cut the **aubergine** lengthways into 1cm slices. Rinse the **lentils** in cold water.

**2** Rub 2 tbsp **olive oil** into the **aubergine** slices, put them on a baking tray in a single layer and season each one with a bit of **salt** (less than ¼ tsp) and a grind of **black pepper**. Grill for 8–9 mins on each side, until browned and soft. Keep an eye on them to make sure they don't burn. If they aren't soft after this time, just leave them under your grill for a little longer. Remove and set aside.

**3** Meanwhile, make the **tomato sauce**. Heat 1½ tbsp **olive oil** in a frying pan over a medium heat. Add the **onion**. Cook until soft, about 5 mins. Add the **courgette** and **pepper** with ¼ tsp **salt** and a few grinds of **black pepper**. Cook until soft and slightly browned, about 5 mins. Add the **garlic, oregano, cinnamon stick** and **tomato purée**. Cook for 1 min more.

**4** Next, add the **lentils, Worcestershire sauce**, the crumbled **vegetable stock cube** and **chopped tomatoes**. Refill the tin a third with water, swish it around and pour that in too. Simmer until the lentils are soft (but still have a slight bite to them), 20–25 mins. If the sauce gets too dry, just add a splash of water.

**5** Cut the **ciabatta** widthways into 1cm thick slices, rub a little **olive oil** on each side with your fingers and place them on another baking tray. Pop them under your preheated grill for 2–3 mins on each side, then remove. Cut the remaining **garlic clove** in half and rub across both sides of the **ciabatta** slices.

**6** When the sauce is ready, remove the **cinnamon stick** and transfer the sauce to an ovenproof dish. Layer over the **aubergine** slices and spread the **crème fraîche** out across the top. Grate over the **Italian hard cheese** and add a grind of **black pepper**. Put under your grill for 5 mins, until the **cheese** is golden. Serve in bowls with the **cheat's garlic bread** on the side.

# HONEY-ROASTED FETA
## – WITH CRISPY SWEET POTATOES & GARLICKY LENTILS –

**READY IN 30 MINS**　　　　　**SERVES** (2)

Down at the HelloFresh Farm (our London HQ) there aren't that many rules, but on their first day everyone gets told they aren't allowed to eat lunch at their desks. Why? Because we have a 60-seat dining table made out of old scaffolding planks where everyone sits down to chat and meet new people. And what are they all eating? HelloFresh of course! A lot of people cook up a recipe the night before and bring a portion for lunch. This recipe makes a perfect dinner and a dead easy lunch too.

### Ingredients

- 500g sweet potato, 1cm wedges
- olive oil
- 1 echalion shallot (the long one), ½cm dice
- 250g cherry tomatoes, halved widthways
- 2 garlic cloves, finely chopped
- 100g feta, cut into six rectangles
- 1 tin cooked Puy lentils, drained and rinsed
- ½ lemon
- 1 tbsp honey
- 40g rocket leaves
- 4 tbsp pomegranate seeds
- 2 tbsp shelled pistachios
- salt and black pepper

### Here's how...

**1** Preheat your oven to 220°C/Gas Mark 7. Wash and chop your **sweet potato** in half lengthways (no need to peel). Rest the flat part on the board and slice into each half lengthways and at an angle to make 2cm thick wedges. Toss the wedges in 1 tbsp **olive oil**, ½ tsp **salt** and a few grinds of **black pepper**. Lay them flat on a baking tray and roast on the top shelf for around 25–30 mins, or until a little crispy at the edges.

**2** Prep the **shallot**, **tomatoes** and **garlic**. Cut the **feta** into six long rectangles. Drain and rinse the **lentils** in a sieve.

**3** Lay some baking paper in another baking tray. Put the **tomatoes** on one half of the baking tray, coat them in 1 tbsp **olive oil** and season with ¼ tsp **salt** and a few grinds of **black pepper**. Put the **feta** pieces on the other half and very gently coat them in 1 tbsp **olive oil**. Once the wedges have been in your oven for 20 mins, pop the **tomatoes** and **feta** on the middle shelf for the last 5–10 mins of cooking time.

**4** Put a frying pan over a medium heat with 1½ tbsp **olive oil** and the **shallot**. Cook until soft, about 4 mins. Add your **garlic** and cook for 1 more min. Add the **lentils** to the pan along with ¼ tsp **salt** and a few grinds of **black pepper**. Stir well. Warm the **lentils** through for around 3 mins, then remove from the heat.

**5** Squeeze the **lemon juice** into a bowl with 1 tbsp **olive oil**. Add ¼ tsp **salt**, a few grinds of **black pepper** and whisk together with a fork. Once the **sweet potato wedges**, **tomatoes** and **feta** are cooked, remove from the oven and season the **wedges** with ¼ tsp more **salt**. Turn the grill to high. Add the **tomatoes** to your **lentil** mixture, along with the **lemony dressing**. Drizzle the **honey** over the **feta** and pop under the grill for 2 mins.

**6** Spoon the **garlicky lentils** into bowls and top with a handful of **rocket**. Place your **wedges** and **feta** on top (if it breaks up don't worry, it will still be delish). Sprinkle over the **pomegranate seeds** and **pistachios** to serve.

# – A SNEAKY –
# COURGETTE & SUN-DRIED TOMATO TART

There is a lot of pride and merit in spending hours in the kitchen perfecting an artisanal dish. That said, these days you can get some really great ready-made puff pastry that'll save you a heap of time and leave you with a result that will leave everyone amazed at your pastry prowess. We've even got it on good authority that a lot of top restaurants craftily take this shortcut too. We won't tell if you don't.

**READY IN 35 MINS**

**SERVES** ②

## Ingredients

- 1 courgette, ½cm discs
- 2 tbsp sun-dried tomatoes, finely chopped
- 2 vine tomatoes, ½cm slices
- olive oil
- 4 tbsp cream cheese
- 2 tbsp hard Italian cheese (i.e. veggie Parmesan), grated
- 2 tbsp milk
- 1 sheet (320g) all-butter puff pastry
- 1 tsp dried oregano
- 40g rocket leaves
- salt and black pepper

## Here's how...

**1** Preheat your oven to 200°C/Gas Mark 6. Prep the **courgette**, **sun-dried tomatoes** and **vine tomatoes**.

**2** Heat a large non-stick frying pan over a high heat. In a bowl mix the **courgette** slices gently with 2 tsp **olive oil**. Fry the **courgettes** for 1 min on each side and remove to a plate. Do not overcrowd the pan – space the **courgettes** out to brown them off.

**3** Mix the **cream cheese** with the **sun-dried tomatoes** and half the grated **hard Italian cheese**. To loosen up the **cheese** add 1 tbsp **milk**.

**4** Unroll the **pastry** onto a lightly greased baking tray and, using a kitchen knife, lightly mark a 1cm border around the edge of it.

**5** Spread the **cream cheese mixture** inside the border. Place the **courgette** and **tomato** slices on top of the tart and scatter over the **oregano**. Brush the **pastry** border with **milk** and sprinkle on ¼ tsp **salt** and a few good grinds of **black pepper**.

**6** Bake for 15–20 mins until the **pastry** has risen and is golden.

**7** Mix your **rocket** with 2 tsp of your best-quality **olive oil**, ¼ tsp **salt** and a few grinds of **black pepper**.

**8** Scatter the **rocket** and remaining **hard Italian cheese** over the cooked **tart** and serve it straight away. **Tip: We like serving one large tart to cut at the table but you can make mini ones of you like.**

# MEDITERRANEAN ALMOND & AUBERGINE STEW
## – WITH FETA & GREEN OLIVES –

Whilst you can have this on the table in no time, it's also one of those dishes that only gets better for having marinated overnight. I tend to make a big batch of this on a Sunday and pack it into individual freezer bags ready for lunches or last-minute dinners during the week. The beauty of the couscous is that you can make it with nothing more than a bowl, a lid and a kettle, so it's a perfect mid-week saviour.

**READY IN 40 MINS**

**SERVES** (2)

## Ingredients

1 vegetable stock pot

2 garlic cloves,
 finely chopped

1 red onion, ½cm dice

1 leek, ½cm half moons

150g couscous

1 aubergine, 1cm dice

olive oil

1 tbsp tomato purée

300g tomato passata

30g pitted green olives

2 tbsp ground almonds

10g fresh basil leaves,
 roughly chopped, plus a few
 whole basil leaves

50g feta, crumbled

salt and black pepper

## Here's how...

**1** Preheat your oven to 200°C/Gas Mark 6. Boil 300ml water with the **vegetable stock pot** in a saucepan over a high heat. While it comes to the boil, prep the **garlic** and **onion**. Remove the root and dark green part from the **leeks** and prep the remainder.

**2** Once your pan of **stock** is boiling, stir to fully dissolve the **stock pot**. Add the **couscous**, then remove from the heat and cover with a lid. Set it aside until everything else is ready.

**3** Trim the top and bottom off the **aubergine** and discard. Cut the **aubergine** in half lengthways, then slice each half lengthways into 1cm thick slices. Now line up the slices and chop widthways into 1cm dice. Place on a baking tray, drizzle over 2 tbsp **olive oil** and season with ½ tsp **salt**. Toss to coat, then spread out evenly and roast on the top shelf of your oven until soft and brown, 20–25 mins.

**4** Heat 1 tbsp **olive oil** in a frying pan over a medium heat. Add the leek, **garlic** and **onion**. Cook with a lid on until soft, about 7 mins. Stir in the **tomato purée** and **tomato passata**. Turn the heat to medium–low and cook until the **stew** begins to thicken, 5–10 mins.

**5** Add the **green olives**, ¼ tsp **salt** and a few grinds of **black pepper** to the **stew**. Once the **aubergine** is cooked, add to the **stew** along with the **ground almonds**.

**6** Pick the **basil leaves** from their stalks and finely chop (discard the stalks). Take the lid off the **couscous** and fluff it up with a fork. Stir through three-quarters of the chopped **basil**.

**7** Plate up the **basil couscous** with the **almond and aubergine stew** on top. Crumble over the **feta** and sprinkle on a few whole **basil leaves** to serve.

# CHICKEN
## -DISHES-

# PAN-FRIED SPRINGTIME CHICKEN
## – WITH PANCETTA & PEAS –

Picking out our favourite dish is much like asking someone to pick their favourite child. We know it's not nice to have a preference, but we can't help but like some more than others. This particular one is the apple of my eye. A deliciously fresh combination of peas and spring onions combined with chicken and pancetta makes for a balanced meal, which begs for a little glass of something cold on the side. Whatever you do, don't tell the other dishes.

**READY IN 30 MINS**

**SERVES** ②

## Ingredients

- 350g new potatoes, halved lengthways
- 3 spring onions, ½cm discs
- 1 garlic clove, finely chopped
- olive oil
- 100g diced smoked pancetta
- 4 skin-on, boneless chicken thighs
- 1 tbsp cornflour
- ½ chicken stock cube
- 80g frozen peas
- 30ml crème fraîche
- salt and black pepper

## Here's how...

**1** Put a medium pan of water with ½ tsp **salt** over a high heat and bring to the boil. Slice the **potatoes** in half lengthways (no need to peel), then prep the **spring onions** and **garlic**.

**2** Put a non-stick frying pan over a medium heat with 1 tsp **olive oil**. Once it's hot, cook off the **pancetta** until crispy around the edges, 4–5 mins. Remove it from the pan and put it in a bowl, leaving the fat in the pan.

**3** Coat each **chicken thigh** thoroughly in a quarter of the **cornflour**, ¼ tsp **salt** and a few grinds of **black pepper**. With the (now empty) pancetta pan still over a medium heat, lay in the **thighs** and cook for 4 mins on each side.

**4** Move the **chicken** to one side of the pan and add in the **garlic** and the **spring onions**. After 30 seconds add the ½ **chicken stock cube** with 150ml boiling water. Bring this to the boil and give everything a good stir.

**5** Add in your **pancetta** and let the whole thing simmer over a medium–low heat with a lid on for 15 mins. Now you can get cracking with the **potatoes**.

**6** Add the **potatoes** to your boiling water and boil for around 10–15 mins. They're done when you can easily slip a knife through them. Once they are ready just drain them, ready to serve.

**7** Finally, remove the lid from the **chicken** and add in the **frozen peas** for a few mins. Take the pan off the heat and leave to rest for a few mins before stirring through the **crème fraîche**. Serve your **chicken** and **creamy sauce** over your **potatoes** and get stuck in.

# 'STRESS-BUSTING' PAN-FRIED CHICKEN
## – WITH CREAMY LENTILS –

Dinner and stress relief in one neat package. For this recipe you'll be tackling a bit of tenderising. It involves a couple of sheets of clingfilm, a saucepan, a bit of elbow grease and a fair bit of noise. If someone happens to walk into the kitchen while you're bashing the chicken, give them a menacing look for good measure and point towards the washing up.

◐ **READY IN 30 MINS**

**SERVES** ②

## Ingredients

- **1 carrot**, ½cm dice
- **1 stick celery**, ½cm dice
- **1 leek**, ½cm discs
- **½ red chilli**, finely chopped
- **1½ tsp fresh thyme leaves**
- **1½ tbsp fresh sage leaves**, roughly chopped
- **olive oil**
- **2 skin-on chicken breasts**
- **1 tin cooked lentils**, drained and rinsed
- **½ chicken stock cube**
- **4 tbsp crème fraîche**
- **salt and black pepper**

## Here's how...

**1** Prep the **carrot** and **celery**. Remove the root and dark green part from the **leek** and prep the **leek**. If you prefer less spice, halve the **chilli** lengthways and scrape out the seeds before finely chopping the **chilli** flesh.

**2** Pinch the top of each **thyme** stalk in one hand and run the thumb and index finger of the other hand downwards to strip off the **leaves**. Pick the **sage leaves** from their stalks and roughly chop. Discard the stalks from both herbs.

**3** Heat 1½ tbsp **olive oil** in a large saucepan over a medium heat. Add the **carrot**, **celery**, **leek**, **chilli**, **thyme** and **sage**. Season with ¼ tsp **salt** and cook gently until soft, about 8 mins. Turn the heat down if the ingredients start to brown.

**4** Place each **chicken breast** between two sheets of clingfilm. Whack with the bottom of a saucepan until just under 1cm thick all over. Heat 1 tbsp **olive oil** in a frying pan over a medium–high heat. Add the **chicken**, skin-side down, and cook for around 3–4 mins on each side. Season each **breast** with a bit of **salt** (less than ¼ tsp) and a few grinds of **black pepper** whilst cooking. The **chicken** is cooked when it is no longer pink in the middle.

**5** Turn the heat to low and thoroughly rinse and drain the **lentils**. Add them to the pan of veggies with 4 tbsp water, the **stock cube** and the **crème fraîche**. Add a few grinds of **black pepper**, taste and add more if needed. Stir well and heat through until the **lentils** are hot.

**6** Spoon the **spicy lentils** onto plates and top with your **pan-fried chicken**.

# CRISPY SKIN CHICKEN
## – WITH BUTTERY BASIL COURGETTES –

🌓 **READY IN 30 MINS**                    **SERVES** ②

To use a much-loved analogy, HelloFresh is a bit like a swan: chefs working calmly on the surface, and legs beneath pumping with all their might. Those 'legs' include our ingredient sourcing team, who will often turn up gleefully holding some strange new ingredient and tell the chefs to get inventive. In this case it was a box of funny little squashes called patty pans. Mimi whipped up this recipe, but to make sure you can cook it at home she's swapped out patty pans for courgettes. It's a corker.

*Ingredients*

- 100g cracked bulgur wheat
- ½ chicken stock cube
- 2 skin-on chicken breasts
- olive oil
- 1 leek, ½cm half moons
- 1 courgette, ½cm discs
- 20g fresh basil, roughly chopped
- 30g butter
- 100g feta
- salt and black pepper

*Here's how...*

**1** Preheat your oven to 200°C/Gas Mark 6. Put the **bulgur wheat** into a pan with 250ml water and crumble in your ½ **stock cube**. Bring to a boil, cover with a lid, then remove from the heat and leave it off the heat for 20 mins, or until the rest of the meal is ready.

**2** Season each **chicken breast** on both sides with ¼ tsp **salt** and a few grinds of **black pepper**. Heat 1 tbsp **olive oil** in a frying pan over a medium–high heat and, once it's really hot, lay in the **chicken**, skin-side down. Cook until the skin is golden, 5–6 mins, then turn over and cook for 1 more min. Transfer to a baking tray (skin-side up) and roast in your oven for 15 mins, until cooked through and no longer pink in the middle. Once cooked, remove from your oven and leave to rest for 5 mins. Don't wash up your frying pan.

**3** Meanwhile, remove the root and dark green part from the **leek** and prep the **leek** and **courgette**. Pull the **basil leaves** off their stalks. Finely chop the **basil stalks**. Finely chop half the **basil leaves** and roughly chop the other half. Keep these **basil** parts separate.

**4** Mix the **finely chopped basil leaves** with 2 tbsp **olive oil**, ¼ tsp **salt** and a few grinds of **black pepper**. This is your **basil oil**.

**5** Take the frying pan you used earlier and add the **butter** over a medium heat. Once melted, add the **leek** and **basil stalks** and cook until softened, 3 mins. Add the **courgette**, ¼ tsp **salt** and a few grinds of **black pepper**. Cook until soft, stirring occasionally, 8 mins.

**6** When the 8 mins are up, remove the veggies pan from the heat and add your **roughly chopped basil**. Crumble in the **feta** and gently stir it through your veggies. When your **bulgur wheat** is cooked, fluff it up with a fork. Taste and add more **salt** and **black pepper** if you feel it needs it.

**7** Once your **chicken** is cooked and rested, put it on a chopping board and cut it into slices about 1cm wide. Serve your **bulgur wheat** in large bowls with your **buttery veggies**, **chicken** and your **basil oil** drizzled over.

# Hello
## INFUSED OIL

Why stop at basil oil? Using fresh herbs like chopped coriander and parsley, or the flavours of fresh chilli and lemon zest, you can make all sorts of infused oils to drizzle onto your dinner.

# RECORD-BREAKING CHICKEN, CHORIZO & VEG-PACKED 'PAELLA'

I was a bit nervous creating a HelloFresh paella; you can't just ride roughshod over a national dish and get away with it. So my first port of call was renowned Spanish chef José Pizarro, the first chef who ever let me cook in his kitchen. Armed with some top tips, I gave it a little HelloFresh twist (which raised some eyebrows) but it soon went top of the recipe leader board for ease and tastiness. Olé!

**READY IN 45 MINS**

**SERVES** (2)

## Ingredients

- 1 **red pepper**, 1cm slices
- 1 **yellow pepper**, 1cm slices
- 2 **garlic cloves**, finely chopped
- 150g **cherry tomatoes**, quartered
- ½ tsp **rosemary leaves**, roughly chopped
- 1 **lemon**, cut into wedges
- 4 skinless, boneless **chicken thighs**, chopped into bite-sized pieces
- 1 **chicken stock pot**
- **olive oil**
- 60g **chorizo**, 1cm dice
- 30g **fresh flat leaf parsley**, finely chopped
- 150g **basmati rice**
- **salt and black pepper**

## Here's how...

**1** Prep the **peppers** and **garlic**. Cut the **cherry tomatoes** into quarters and, on a separate chopping board, cut the **chicken thighs** into bite-sized pieces. Strip the leaves from the **rosemary** and chop them (discarding the stems). Cut the **lemon** into wedges. Pour 300ml boiling water into a jug with the **chicken stock pot** and stir to dissolve.

**2** Heat 1½ tbsp **olive oil** in a frying pan over a high heat. Season your **chicken** with ½ tsp **salt** and a few grinds of **black pepper**. Add your **chicken** to the pan and fry for a few mins. Once brown on all sides, remove and keep to the side.

**3** Add another 1½ tbsp **olive oil** to the frying pan. Add your **peppers** and **tomatoes**. Cook for a few mins until softened. Chop your **chorizo** into 1cm dice. Add your **garlic**, **rosemary leaves** and the **chorizo** to the pan. Prep the **parsley**.

**4** After 3 mins, add the **rice** and half the **parsley**. Cook for a few mins until your **rice** absorbs the oil.

**5** Add your **chicken stock** and **chicken**. Give everything a good stir and put a tight-fitting lid on top. Reduce the heat to medium and cook for 10 mins on the heat and 10 mins off the heat. It's really important you do not touch the lid until at least 20 mins are up or the rice will not cook properly.

**6** Serve the paella with your remaining **parsley** and the **lemon wedges**.

## Hello
## BASMATI

Basmati is usually more common
in your cupboard than paella rice,
so we've tweaked the traditional
recipe so you can cook this
one spontaneously.

# TERIYAKI CHICKEN

## – WITH RICE & PAK CHOI –

🌓 **READY IN 30 MINS**  **SERVES** ②

Life in the kitchen was fairly intense back in the old days. Yours truly would start each week with a blank slate and have to create, test, photograph, write and proofread at least ten new recipes covering all sorts of cuisines and new techniques. 'Chef's block' was a real thing. That's where take-aways provided inspiration, leading me to create healthier, quicker, tastier versions to make at home. This teriyaki was one of those recipes. The take-aways didn't thank us.

*Ingredients*

- 150g white basmati rice
- 4 pak choi, thinly sliced
- 2 garlic cloves, finely chopped
- 2 tbsp fresh ginger, peeled and finely chopped
- 4 skinless, boneless chicken thighs, ½cm slices
- 1½ tbsp coconut milk powder (optional)
- 2 tbsp honey
- 3 tbsp soy sauce
- 50g cashew nuts
- flavourless oil
- salt and black pepper

*Here's how...*

**1** Put a pan over a high heat and bring 300ml water to the boil for the **rice**. Remove the root from the **pak choi** and then cut the rest into thin slices. Prep the **garlic** and **ginger**. Cut the **chicken** into very thin (½cm) slices.

**2** Stir ¼ tsp **salt** into your pan of boiling water (if you have some **coconut milk powder** you can jazz up the **rice** a bit more by adding 1½ tbsp now). Add the **rice** and cover with a lid. Cook for 10 mins over a medium heat, then remove from the heat and leave to rest for 10 mins. Don't peek under the lid until the 20 mins are up.

**3** To make the **teriyaki sauce**, simply mix the **garlic**, **ginger**, **honey** and **soy sauce** together in a bowl.

**4** Put a frying pan over a medium–high heat. Add the **cashews** (no oil). Toast until beginning to brown, 2–3 mins, shaking the pan occasionally. Watch the **nuts** carefully because they can burn really easily. When done, remove from the pan and allow to cool, then roughly chop and set aside.

**5** Put the pan back over a high heat and add 1 tbsp **oil**. When it is almost smoking, add a layer of **chicken**. Cook until brown, 5–7 mins. Repeat with the rest of the **chicken**. Cooking it in batches will mean the pan isn't overcrowded, so the **chicken** will brown instead of stewing.

**6** Once the **chicken** is nicely browned, return all the **chicken** to the pan, reduce the heat to medium and add the **pak choi**. Cook for a further 2–3 mins. Add the teriyaki sauce. Stir together. Cook for a final 2–3 mins until the **chicken** is cooked through and no longer pink in the middle.

**7** Fluff up the **rice** with a fork and serve it with your **teriyaki chicken** and a sprinkling of **cashew nuts**.

# THAI MASSAMAN RICE
## – WITH CRUNCHY PEANUT BUTTER –

**READY IN 35 MINS**　　　　　　　　**SERVES** (2)

This recipe is a shining example of leftovers being even better than the meal from which they came. I'd made a huge batch of massaman curry that even my fellow HelloFresh vultures couldn't polish off. The next day I just mixed up all the leftover rice and curry with a scattering of fresh coriander and voilà! This recipe became a fave – Thai comfort food at its best.

### Ingredients

- 1 carrot, ½cm slices
- 3 tbsp fresh coriander, roughly chopped
- 250g chestnut mushrooms, ½cm slices
- 4 skinless, boneless chicken thighs, 3cm dice
- 150g white basmati rice
- 40g cashew nuts
- olive oil
- 2 tbsp massaman curry paste
- 400ml coconut milk
- 1 chicken stock pot
- ½ tsp fish sauce
- 2 tbsp crunchy peanut butter
- 150g green beans, trimmed and chopped into 1cm pieces
- 2 limes, one in wedges
- ready-made crispy onions
- salt and black pepper

## Here's how...

**1** Put a pan of 300ml water with ¼ tsp **salt** over a high heat and bring to the boil. While the water is coming to the boil, prep the **carrot** and **coriander**. Slice the **mushrooms** and cut up the **chicken**.

**2** Add the **rice** to your pan of boiling water. Cover with a tight lid and keep over a medium heat for 10 mins. Then take the pan off the heat to rest for 10 mins. For perfect **rice** do not lift the lid from the pan at all during cooking and resting.

**3** Put a frying pan over a medium–high heat. Add the **cashews** (no oil). Toast until beginning to brown, 2–3 mins, shaking the pan occasionally. Watch the **nuts** like a hawk because they can burn really easily. When done, remove from the pan and allow to cool. Then roughly chop and set aside.

**4** Add 1 tbsp **oil** to the now empty pan over a high heat. Once the pan is really hot add the **chicken** and cook until golden brown all over, about 5 mins, then remove and set aside. Cook in batches if you have a small pan to avoid it stewing rather than browning.

**5** In the now empty pan, add the **massaman curry paste**. Stir the **paste** for 1 min, then stir in a quarter of the **coconut milk** until the mixture is smooth. Add the **chicken stock pot** and the **fish sauce** and stir to dissolve (add more **fish sauce** to taste, but go slowly).

**6** Now add the remaining **coconut milk**, the **chicken**, the **mushrooms** and the **carrot**. Once the **coconut milk** comes to the boil, stir in the **peanut butter** and turn the heat to low. Simmer gently, until the **chicken** is cooked and no longer pink in the middle, and the **sauce** has darkened and thickened, around 10 mins. Trim the ends from the **green beans**, chop into 1cm pieces, then put them in the pan for the last 3 mins.

**7** Fluff up the **rice** with a fork and add it to the pan of **massaman sauce** along with three-quarters of the chopped **coriander**. Give one of the **limes** a good roll over the bench to get the juices going and then cut it into halves and squeeze over as much juice as you'd like. Cut the other **lime** into wedges. Serve the **massaman rice** in bowls and garnish with the remaining **coriander, cashews, lime wedges** and the **crispy onions**.

### Hello
## CRISPY ONIONS

Ready-made crispy onions are sold in most large supermarkets and will add a beautiful bit of crunch and flavour to your dishes.

# PAN-FRIED CHICKEN
## – WITH NEW POTATOES & TARRAGON SAUCE –

🌓 **READY IN 30 MINS**　　　　　**SERVES** ②

Say hello to our customer catnip: tarragon. This was one of the first recipes I ever cooked using tarragon (in my life, not just for our customers) and it went down a treat. I'm guessing it's because tarragon doesn't feature that highly on the average shopping list and to the uninitiated it may be a little intimidating. As ever though, get a few pointers and away you go. We've got a whole section of our archive dedicated to this little wonder herb now.

### *Ingredients*

- 500g new potatoes, bite-sized pieces
- olive oil
- 150g green beans, trimmed
- 2 tbsp fresh tarragon leaves, finely chopped
- 2 skinless chicken breasts
- 3 tbsp crème fraîche
- 1 tsp Dijon mustard
- salt and black pepper

### *Here's how...*

**1** Preheat your oven to 220°C/Gas Mark 7. Wash and chop the new **potatoes** into bite-sized pieces (no need to peel). Toss the **potatoes** in 1 tbsp **olive oil**, ½ tsp **salt** and a few grinds of **black pepper**. Lay them flat on a baking tray and roast on the top shelf of the oven for around 25–30 mins, or until a little crispy at the edges.

**2** Trim the very ends from the **green beans** and discard. Pick the **tarragon leaves** from their stalks and finely chop (discard the stalks).

**3** Lay each **chicken breast** between two sheets of clingfilm on a chopping board and bash it with a rolling pin or the base of a pan until it is 1cm thick.

**4** Heat 1 tbsp **olive oil** in a frying pan over a medium–high heat. Season each **chicken breast** on both sides with ¼ tsp **salt** and a couple of grinds of **black pepper**. Once the **oil** is hot, cook the **chicken** for 3–4 mins on each side, until cooked through and no longer pink in the middle. Remove the pan from the heat and set aside.

**5** Bring a large saucepan of water to the boil with 1 tsp **salt** and add the **green beans**. Boil for 3 mins then drain and set aside (we like ours with a bit of crunch left in the middle).

**6** Put the frying pan back over a low heat. Add the **crème fraîche**, 3 tbsp water and the **Dijon mustard**. Bubble gently until you have the consistency of double cream, then return the **chicken** to the pan. Remove from the heat, then stir in the **tarragon**. Serve your **potatoes** and **beans** alongside the **chicken** with a healthy spoonful of your ~~catnip~~ **tarragon sauce**.

# HELLOFRESH TANDOORI TAKE-DOWN
## – WITH HERB-INFUSED RICE –

**READY IN 35 MINS**  **SERVES** (2)

Why should tandoori restaurants have the monopoly on melt-in-your-mouth tender chicken? We sent our Curry Research Unit on a mission and they came back with a bellyful of inspiration. One of the magic ingredients is cornflour. In 'the trade' they call this magical ingredient a tenderiser, but the science is quite simple: by coating the chicken you seal in more of the moisture for a totally succulent result.

*Ingredients*

- 1 chicken stock pot
- 150g brown basmati rice
- 1 red onion, ½cm half moons
- 1 yellow pepper, 1cm strips
- 1 garlic clove, finely chopped
- 3 tbsp fresh coriander, roughly chopped
- 2 skinless chicken breasts, chopped into bite-sized pieces
- 1 tbsp cornflour
- flavourless oil
- 1½ tbsp jalfrezi spice mix
- 1 tin chopped tomatoes
- ½ lemon
- 100ml crème fraîche
- salt and black pepper

*Here's how...*

**1** Put a medium pan of water over a high heat and bring to the boil with ½ the **chicken stock pot**. Put the **rice** in a sieve and rinse under running water for at least 30 seconds. Cook the rice until soft (lid off), 25 mins. Drain the **rice** in your sieve and put it back in the empty pan, off the heat, covering it with a tea towel.

**2** Prep the **onion, yellow pepper** and **garlic**. Separate the **coriander** leaves from their stems, and roughly chop both the leaves and stems (but keep separate). Chop the **chicken** into bite-sized pieces.

**3** Mix the **cornflour** with ½ tsp **salt** and a few grinds of **black pepper**. Coat your **chicken** thoroughly in the **cornflour**. Heat 1 tbsp **oil** in a large frying pan over a medium–high heat. Once hot, add your **chicken** and cook until brown on all sides, about 5 mins. No need to cook it all the way through as we'll do that later in the recipe.

**4** Remove the **chicken** from the pan and turn the heat to medium. Add 1 tbsp **oil** and the **yellow pepper** and fry for 3 mins, then add the **onion** and fry for a further 2 mins, or until soft. Finally add the **garlic, coriander stalks** and **jalfrezi spice** and cook for a final min.

**5** Add the **chicken, tomatoes**, remainder of the **chicken stock pot** and 50ml water to your pan. Turn the heat to low, stir together and allow to bubble away for 10–15 mins, until the **chicken** is cooked through and no longer pink in the middle. To finish, squeeze in the **lemon juice** and stir in half the **crème fraîche**. Season with **salt** and **black pepper** to taste.

**6** Spoon the **rice** into bowls and top with the **curry**, the **crème fraîche** and a sprinkling of your **coriander leaves**. Savour the succulence!

### Hello
SPICE

We use a spice mix from
Seasoned Pioneers (you can
order online), but failing that,
look for a tandoori spice mix.

# WILD MUSHROOM TAGLIATELLE
## – WITH CHICKEN & FRESH TARRAGON –

Apparently, opportunities are like London buses – you wait ages for one to come along and then they all arrive at once. When we started HelloFresh I was also asked to film a cooking show around Italy. Faced with two amazing adventures, I did the sensible thing: drank a lot more coffee and did both. I fell in love with northern Italy during that time and the flavours of this dish are inspired by the beautiful Marche region.

**READY IN 30 MINS**

**SERVES** (2)

## Ingredients

- 1 **red onion**, ½cm dice
- 1 **garlic clove**, finely chopped
- 3 tbsp fresh flat leaf **parsley**, finely chopped
- 1½ tbsp fresh **tarragon leaves**, finely chopped
- 150g **wild mushrooms** (get a mix), roughly chopped
- 1 **chicken stock cube**
- 3 skinless, boneless **chicken thighs**
- **olive oil**
- 1½ tsp **plain flour**
- 200g **tagliatelle**
- 3 tbsp **crème fraîche**
- 1 **lemon**
- 2 tbsp **Parmesan**, grated
- **salt** and **black pepper**

## Here's how...

**1** Preheat your oven to 180°C/Gas Mark 4 and boil a small amount of water in the kettle. Prep the **red onion**, **garlic** and **parsley**. Strip the leaves from the **tarragon** stalk, finely chop the leaves and discard the stalk. Roughly chop the **mushrooms** and mix the **stock cube** with 50ml boiling water.

**2** Coat each of the **chicken thighs** in 1 tsp **olive oil**, ¼ tsp **salt** and a grind of **black pepper**. Place them on a baking tray and cook on the top shelf of the oven for 25 mins, until cooked through and no longer pink in the middle.

**3** Heat a large frying pan over a medium heat and add 1 tbsp **olive oil**. Add the **red onion** and cook gently (AKA 'sweating' the **onions**) for 5 mins until soft and translucent. Add the **garlic** and **mushrooms** and season with ¼ tsp **salt** and a few grinds of **black pepper**. Cook for 5 mins until the **mushrooms** are cooked through, then turn the heat to low.

**4** Bring a large pan of water with 1 tbsp **salt** to the boil for the pasta. While the water comes to the boil, sprinkle the **flour** over the **mushrooms**, stir gently and cook for 1 min.

**5** Cook your **tagliatelle** in the boiling water for around 10 mins or until 'al dente' (cooked through but with a tiny bit of firmness left in the middle).

**6** Add the **stock**, **parsley** and **tarragon** to the pan containing the **mushrooms**. Simmer gently until thickened, about 3 mins. Add a few tbsp of the **pasta water** to loosen it up.

**7** Turn the heat to medium–low and stirr in the **crème fraîche**. Add 2 tbsp **lemon juice** and a couple more twists of **black pepper** and cook gently for 1–2 mins.

**8** Mix the **pasta** in the pan with the **sauce**, chop the **chicken** into small pieces and add this too. Serve with a sprinkle of the grated **Parmesan**.

# WHOLEGRAIN MUSTARD POTATO SALAD
## – WITH GRILLED CHICKEN –

🌓 **READY IN 25 MINS**                    **SERVES** ②

Writing the story for this recipe, it would have been easy to talk about how salads often seem like a punishment for our weekend excesses and how this dish proves that wrong. But when our chef Dominique cooked it up she said in no uncertain terms that it was so tasty, the story should be entirely positive. She says it reminds her of an al fresco lunch in the Scandinavian fjords and wouldn't be inappropriately matched with a nice, crisp rosé. Who are we to argue?

*Ingredients*

- 350g new potatoes, 2cm dice
- 3 spring onions, ½cm half moons
- 1 stick celery, finely chopped
- 150g green beans, trimmed and halved
- 2 skinless chicken breasts
- olive oil
- 100ml soured cream
- 3 tbsp fresh flat leaf parsley, roughly chopped
- 1 tsp wholegrain mustard
- 1 lemon, zest and juice
- 2 tsp red wine vinegar
- salt and black pepper

*Here's how...*

**1** Put a large pan of water with ½ tsp **salt** over a high heat and bring to the boil. Prep the **potatoes** (no need to peel), add to your pan of boiling water and boil until tender, about 10 mins. They should be soft enough to eat, but not cooked so much that they're mushy. Prep the **spring onions** and **celery**. Trim the ends from the **green beans**, then cut the **green beans** in half.

**2** On a separate chopping board, lay the **chicken breasts** between two sheets of clingfilm. Whack the **chicken** with a rolling pin or the base of a pan until it is 1cm thick.

**3** Put 1 tbsp **olive oil** in a frying pan over a medium–high heat. Season each **chicken breast** on both sides with ¼ tsp **salt** and a few grinds of **black pepper**. Once the pan is hot, fry the **chicken** for 3–4 mins on each side until cooked through and no longer pink in the middle, then remove from the pan and leave to rest for 5 mins.

**4** Once your **potatoes** are cooked, remove them from the pan with a slotted spoon and put them aside to cool for a few mins. Keep the pan of water boiling and use it to cook the **green beans** until tender with a little bit of bite left, 2 mins only. When cooked, drain the **beans** in a colander and put them in a bowl of cold water to stop them going soft. This helps to keep that gorgeous crunch.

**5** Mix all your **dressing** ingredients in a small bowl (**soured cream**, **parsley**, **mustard**, the **zest** of the whole **lemon**, the **juice** of half the **lemon** and the **vinegar**). When the **potatoes** have cooled down pour over the dressing and add the **celery**, **beans** and **spring onions**, then gently fold it all together.

**6** Pile your salad on a plate, slice your **chicken** at an angle and place it across the top. Finish with a final squeeze of **lemon juice** for freshness. Välsmakande! (That's 'tasty' in Swedish.)

# LEEK & MUSTARD CHICKEN

**READY IN 35 MINS**          **SERVES** ②

It's fair to say that our Mimi is a bit of a character. When I asked her about this recipe she said she wasn't entirely sure her story would be appropriate, but here goes…Apparently, Mimi first came up with this recipe on a hot day at home. In fact it was so hot that she decided to dispel with her clothes during the cooking process. Imagine then the look on the estate agent's face when he let himself in to show new tenants around. Dinnertime!

## Ingredients

- **1 leek**, thin half moons
- **450g potatoes**, peeled and cut into 4cm dice
- **150g green beans**, trimmed
- **olive oil**
- **2 skin-on chicken breasts**
- **100ml double cream**
- **1 tbsp wholegrain mustard**
- **2 tsp butter**
- **2 tbsp milk**
- **½ tsp mustard seeds**
- **salt and black pepper**

## Here's how…

**1** Put a medium pan of water with ½ tsp **salt** over a high heat and bring to the boil.

**2** Remove the root and dark green part from the leek and prep the **leek** and **potatoes**. Trim the ends from the **green beans** and discard. Put your **potatoes** in the pan of boiling water and cook for roughly 20 mins, then drain, pop back into your pan and cover with a lid. The **potatoes** are cooked when you can easily slip a knife through.

**3** Heat 1½ tbsp **olive oil** in a frying pan over a medium heat, add the **leeks** with ¼ tsp **salt** and a few grinds of **black pepper**. Cook until soft, 5 mins. Remove them to a plate. Season each **chicken breast** with a bit of **salt** (less than ¼ tsp) and a few grinds of **black pepper**. Add 1 tbsp **olive oil** to your frying pan (still over a medium heat) and cook the chicken until the outside is brown and the inside is cooked, 7–8 mins on each side. The **chicken** is cooked when it is no longer pink in the middle.

**4** When your **chicken** is cooked, add the **double cream** to the pan along with the **wholegrain mustard**, **leeks** and 2 tbsp water. Stir, then cook for another 3 mins until everything is combined and hot. Spoon a little of your creamy sauce over your **chicken** and set the pan aside, covering it with a lid to keep your **chicken** warm.

**5** Add ¼ tsp **salt** and a few grinds of **black pepper** to the **potatoes** in their pan, along with the **butter** and **milk**. Mash with a potato masher or the back of a fork. Cover with a lid and set aside until ready to serve.

**6** Heat 1 tbsp **olive oil** in another frying pan over a medium heat. Add the **mustard seeds** and cook for 30 seconds (careful they don't jump out), then add the **green beans** along with a bit of **salt** (less than ¼ tsp) and a few grinds of **black pepper**. Cook until slightly softened, 3 mins, then add 3 tbsp water to the pan, cover with a lid and cook for 4 more mins.

**7** When everything is ready, stir 2 tbsp water into your **creamy chicken sauce** if the liquid has evaporated too much. Take your **chicken** out of the pan and slice into 2cm slices. Serve your **chicken** with your **mash**, your stir-fried **green beans** and a good helping of **sauce**.

# POPPY SEED-CRUSTED CHICKEN
## – WITH CREAMY RIGATONI & PEAS –

**READY IN 45 MINS**　　　　　**SERVES** ②

Since the dawn of HelloFresh time, I've been campaigning to get more peas on the menu. The struggle has been real. On the one hand you had me wanting to 'give peas a chance', whilst on the other hand there was Luke often having to spend his weekends shelling them and his desire to maintain his soft hands meant there were often heated debates over adding them to a dish. When I was considering this recipe for the book it didn't have peas. So I added some. Just don't tell Luke.

### Ingredients

- 2 skinless chicken breasts
- olive oil
- ½ tsp thyme leaves, finely chopped
- 200g rigatoni pasta
- 100g frozen peas
- 1 leek, ½cm discs
- 1 garlic clove, finely chopped
- 1 chicken stock pot
- 170ml double cream
- ½ tsp Dijon mustard
- 125g baby spinach
- 30g panko breadcrumbs
- 1 tsp poppy seeds
- 40g Parmesan, grated
- salt and black pepper

*Here's how...*

**1** Preheat your oven to 200°C/Gas Mark 6 and put a large pan of water over a high heat to boil. Put the **chicken** in a bowl, season with ½ tsp **salt** and a good grind of **black pepper** and drizzle over 1 tbsp **olive oil**. Pull the leaves from the **thyme** and roughly chop (discard the stems). Mix half the **thyme** with the **chicken**.

**2** Heat a frying pan over a high heat with 2 tbsp olive oil. When the pan is hot, carefully lay your **chicken** in the pan and cook for 2 mins on each side until golden brown on both sides. Transfer your **chicken** to a deep-sided baking dish and pop it in the oven for 10 mins. Don't wash the frying pan as we'll use it later.

**3** When your pan of water comes to the boil, add 1 tsp **salt** along with the **rigatoni** and cook for 11 mins, or according to the packet instructions, until 'al dente' (cooked through but with a tiny bit of firmness left in the middle). For the last 3 mins add in your **frozen peas**. When your **pasta** and **peas** are cooked, drain into a colander and then return to the pan off the heat. Toss in 1 tsp **olive oil** to stop it all sticking together.

**4** As your **chicken** and **pasta** cook, remove the root and dark green part from the leek and prep the **leek** and **garlic**. Reheat the frying pan you used earlier over a medium heat and add ½ tbsp **olive oil**. Add your chopped **leek** and cook for 7 mins or until softened. Add your **garlic** and leftover **thyme leaves** and cook for 1 min more.

**5** Add the **chicken stock pot** with 150ml water and bring to the boil. Pour in the **double cream** and **mustard** and bring your **sauce** back up to a gentle bubble. Taste and add more **salt** and **black pepper** if necessary. Mix with your **pasta** and add the **baby spinach**.

**6** Next, make the crust. Mix the **breadcrumbs** with the **poppy seeds**, grated Parmesan and 1 tbsp olive oil.

**7** Preheat your grill to high. Remove your **chicken** from the baking dish and leave it to rest for at least 3 mins (important). Cut the **chicken** into ½cm slices, then return it to the baking tray and mix together with your **pasta** and sauce. Sprinkle your **poppy seed crust** all over. Put the tray bake under the grill and cook for 2–3 mins or until golden brown.

# SINGAPORE LAKSA

## – WITH CRISPY CHICKEN THIGHS & KAFFIR LIME –

**READY IN 40 MINS**    **SERVES** 2

Sometimes creativity comes from the most unlikely places. This recipe was inspired by a dish we tried in Singapore airport of all places. Trust me. This isn't your regular transit fare. The restaurant was tucked away from the more commercial offerings and packed full of locals: always a sure sign that you're in for something special.

### Ingredients

- 2 spring onions, ½cm discs
- 1 garlic clove, finely chopped
- 1 tbsp fresh ginger, peeled and finely chopped
- 3 tbsp fresh coriander, finely chopped
- 1 lime, zest and juice
- flavourless oil
- 1 tbsp red curry paste
- 400ml coconut milk
- 1 chicken stock pot
- ½–1 tsp fish sauce
- 2 dried kaffir lime leaves
- 1½ tbsp crunchy peanut butter
- 4 skinless, boneless chicken thighs
- 2 nests medium-size egg noodles
- sugar (optional)
- 30g beansprouts
- salt and black pepper

## Here's how...

**1** Prep the **spring onions** (you can keep the green parts aside for a garnish if you like), **garlic**, **ginger** and **coriander**, and zest your **lime**.

**2** Heat 1 tbsp **oil** over a medium heat in a large saucepan. Add the **garlic**, **ginger** and three-quarters of the **spring onions**. After 1 min add the **red curry paste** (add less if you don't like spice) and stir. After another min add the **coconut milk** and stir until smooth. Add the **chicken stock pot** and **fish sauce** with 200ml water then bring to a simmer. Finally add the **kaffir lime leaves** and the **peanut butter**. Leave it to simmer while you seal your **chicken**.

**3** Trim any fatty bits from the **chicken** and season both sides of each **thigh** with ¼ tsp **salt**. Heat 1 tbsp **oil** in a frying pan over a medium–high heat. Once hot, add the **chicken** and cook for a couple of mins on each side to brown. Add to the **laksa**, pop a lid on and let it gently poach the **chicken** for 5 mins.

**4** When the **chicken** is nearly done, add in the **egg noodles** with 200ml more water (or until the **noodles** are covered). Cook until soft enough to eat, about 4 mins. Roll the **lime** firmly under the heel of your hand on the chopping board to loosen up the juices, then cut it in half and squeeze half the **lime juice** into the **laksa**, as well as the **zest** from earlier. Now taste and see what you think it needs – **salt**, **black pepper**, more **lime juice**, **fish sauce** or **sugar** – whatever suits you.

**5** Finally, take the **chicken** out of the pan and chop it into ½cm slices. Serve the **laksa** in big bowls topped with the **chicken strips**, **coriander**, **beansprouts** and the remaining **spring onions**, along with any other toppings you love.

## Hello
## TOPPINGS

We sometimes add a dash of shichimi togarashi, a spicy Japanese chilli powder.

# OUR CLASSIC CHICKEN CURRY
## – WITH HERBY RICE & FLAKED ALMONDS –

When I tasted this recipe, I threw my hands up in praise. It was as if I'd been transported to my favourite tandoori. At that point I had to know who'd created the recipe. My first lead: Chef Mimi. But upon further investigation Chef André disclosed that he'd given it a tweak or two. Then, just as I thought I'd got to the bottom of the matter, our very own Lizzie took me aside and claimed ultimate credit. I'll just diplomatically say, 'Great team effort guys!'

🕐 **READY IN 40 MINS**

**SERVES** ②

## *Ingredients*

- 1 chicken stock pot
- 150g white basmati rice
- 1 onion, 1cm dice
- 3 tbsp fresh coriander, roughly chopped
- 150g green beans, trimmed and cut into 3 pieces
- 1 tsp fresh ginger, peeled and very finely chopped
- 2 skinless chicken breasts, chopped into 2cm dice
- 3 tbsp flaked almonds
- flavourless oil
- 1½ tsp curry powder
- 4 tbsp mango chutney
- 50g raisins
- 150ml double cream
- salt and black pepper

## *Here's how...*

**1** Put a pan of 300ml water over a high heat and bring to the boil. Stir in half the **chicken stock pot** until it dissolves, then add the **rice**. Stir and return to the boil, pop a lid on the pan, reduce the heat to medium–low and simmer for 10 mins. When the 10 mins are up, remove the pan from the heat and leave to the side for another 10 mins. For perfectly cooked **rice** don't touch the lid until 20 mins are up.

**2** Prep the **onion**, **coriander**, **green beans**, **ginger** and **chicken**.

**3** Heat a frying pan over a medium–high heat with no oil, add the **flaked almonds** and fry until golden brown. Remove and keep to the side.

**4** Put 1 tbsp **oil** in your (now empty) pan. Add the **onion** and cook, stirring occasionally, until soft, 5 mins. Add the **chicken**, **ginger** and **curry powder** and cook, stirring, for 1 min to combine. Reduce the heat to medium–low, stir in half the **mango chutney**, the **raisins**, **double cream**, remaining half **chicken stock pot** and 150ml water. Season with ¼ tsp **salt** and a few grinds of **black pepper**.

**5** Bring the **curry** to a gentle simmer, stirring occasionally, until thick and creamy and the **chicken** is cooked and no longer pink in the middle, 8–10 mins. Halfway through cooking, stir in the **green beans**.

**6** When the **curry** is cooked, stir through half the chopped **coriander**, taste and add more **salt** and **black pepper** if you feel it needs it. If you like things a little sweeter, stir through the remaining **mango chutney** – this is how we like it (if not, you can serve some on the side). Fluff up the **rice** with a fork.

**7** Stir the remaining **coriander** through the **rice** and serve it in bowls topped with plenty of **chicken curry** and a scattering of **flaked almonds**.

# MEXICAN CHICKEN & TOMATO JUMBLE
## – WITH NIGELLA YOGHURT –

🕐 **READY IN 35 MINS**                    **SERVES** ②

Mexican food in London used to be fairly run-of-the-mill taco territory, but when Wahaca opened things got exciting. With HelloFresh only a year old, we did our first 'celeb chef recipe' with Thomasina Miers, Wahaca's founder. We filmed it ourselves and everything was going really well until we got to the end of the recipe and I realised I hadn't turned on the microphone. I blamed the equipment, Tommi pretended she believed me and we did another take. We're dedicating this creation to her for being such a good sport.

### Ingredients

- 600g sweet potato, 2cm dice
- olive oil
- 4 tbsp fresh coriander, roughly chopped
- 250g cherry tomatoes (mix of red and yellow if poss), halved lengthways
- 2 skinless chicken breasts
- ½ tsp fajita spice mix
- 1 lime, zest and juice
- 100g feta, crumbled
- 1 courgette, shaved into ribbons
- 2 tbsp Greek yoghurt
- 2 tsp nigella seeds
- salt and black pepper

### *Here's how...*

**1** Preheat your oven to 220°C/Gas Mark 7. Wash and prep the **sweet potato** (no need to peel).

**2** Toss the **sweet potato** in 2 tbsp **olive oil**, 1 tsp **salt** and a few grinds of **black pepper**. Place on a baking tray in a single layer and cook on the top shelf of the oven for 20–25 mins, until crispy around the edges.

**3** Prep the **coriander** and cut the **cherry tomatoes** in half lengthways. On a new chopping board, place your hand flat on top of the **chicken breasts** and slice into the middle. Slice nearly all the way through so that you can open up the **chicken** like a book. You have just 'butterflied' your **chicken**.

**4** Mix the **fajita spice mix** with the **zest** of the whole **lime** and 1 tbsp **olive oil**. Roll the **lime** firmly under the heel of your hand on the chopping board to loosen up its juices and then cut it in half and squeeze 1 tsp **juice** into the mixture along with ¼ tsp **salt** and a few grinds of **black pepper**.

**5** Rub the mixture over the **chicken breasts**. Heat 1 tbsp **olive oil** in a frying pan over a medium–high heat. Fry the **chicken** for 4–5 mins on both sides. The **chicken** is cooked when it is no longer pink in the middle. Once it's cooked, let it rest off the heat for a few mins and then slice it into 1cm strips.

**6** Toss the **tomatoes** with the **juice** of half the **lime**, ¼ tsp **salt** and some **black pepper**. Crumble in the **feta** using your fingers. Toss in the **coriander** and the **sweet potato**. Pile the mixture onto plates and top with the **chicken slices**. Use a vegetable peeler to shave lengthways ribbons from your **courgette** and pile the **courgette ribbons** on top of the **chicken** with the **yoghurt** and **nigella seeds**.

# TURMERIC CHICKEN
## – WITH SRI LANKAN SPICED COURGETTE RICE –

**READY IN 35 MINS**       **SERVES** 2

We couldn't very well tell you that we go in search of the best recipes and the most delicious ingredients if we just sat in our kitchen all day looking through cookbooks and surfing the interweb. That's why I decided to go on a trip to Sri Lanka. I cooked this recipe on a cinnamon plantation after learning the (surprising) secret to preparing cinnamon sticks from an 87-year-old local pro named Ari. You can see the videos on our YouTube page by searching for HelloFreshUK.

### Ingredients

- 1 onion, ½cm dice
- 1 garlic clove, finely chopped
- 1 courgette, 1cm dice
- ½ red chilli, finely chopped
- 4 tbsp fresh coriander, roughly chopped
- flavourless oil
- ½ tbsp fennel seeds
- 1½ tsp ground coriander
- 1½ tsp ground cumin
- ¾ tsp ground turmeric
- 150g white basmati rice
- 1 chicken stock pot
- 1 cinnamon stick
- 4 skin-on, boneless chicken thighs
- 2 tbsp desiccated coconut
- 4 tbsp natural yoghurt
- salt and black pepper

### Here's how...

**1** Prep the **onion**, **garlic**, **courgette** and **red chilli**. Separate the **coriander leaves** and **stalks** . Finely chop the **stalks** and finely chop the **leaves** (but keep them separate).

**2** Put a medium pan over a medium heat with 1½ tbsp **oil**. Add the **onion** and cook for 5 mins until softened, stirring occasionally. Add the **garlic**, **chilli** (less if you don't like spice), **fennel seeds**, **ground coriander**, **cumin** and half the **turmeric**. Cook together for 1 min. Add the **rice** to your pan along with the **courgette** and **coriander stalks**. Stir so the **rice** is nicely coated in the spices.

**3** Pour in 300ml water and add the **chicken stock pot** and **cinnamon stick**. Stir together to dissolve the **stock pot** and bring to a gentle boil. Once boiling, put the lid on and leave to cook for 10 mins. Once the 10 mins is up, remove from the heat and leave for another 10 mins. Don't touch the lid until at least 20 mins are up.

**4** Mix half the **coriander leaves** with your remaining **turmeric** and 2 tbsp **oil** in a bowl. Add the **chicken thighs** to the bowl and season with ½ tsp **salt** and a few grinds of **black pepper**. Mix together so the **chicken** is nicely coated in the mixture. Heat a frying pan over a medium–high heat and add the **dessicated coconut**. Stir and toast until golden, 1–2 mins. Remove from the pan.

**5** Wipe out your pan and pop it back over a medium–high heat. Once hot, cook the **chicken** in your pan skin-side down for 4–5 mins. Turn and cook for another 8 mins, until the **chicken** is cooked through and no longer pink in the middle. Once cooked, remove the **chicken** to a board to rest for 2 mins.

**6** Remove the **cinnamon stick** from the **rice** and fluff it up with a fork. Stir through half the remaining **coriander leaves** and half the **toasted coconut**. Stir the remaining **coconut** into the **yoghurt**. Slice the **chicken** into 2cm wide pieces. Spoon the **rice** onto plates and place the **chicken** on top. Finish with the **coconut yoghurt** and a sprinkle of **coriander** to serve.

### Hello
### CHICKEN

You might have to buy thighs with the bone in and take them out yourself. If you don't fancy doing this, then you can always buy skin-off, bone-out thighs.

# GOBBLE-UP TURKEY* STIR-FRY
## – WITH RICE –

🕐 **READY IN 20 MINS**　　　　　**SERVES** ② 

Lights, camera, action! I saw Chef André whip up this stir-fry in 20 minutes flat whilst we hosted a Facebook Live cook-a-long. If he can do it under the glare of the cameras then you'll have it on the table in no time. Coconut milk powder is a great little addition to the recipe. If you can't find it in a store then order some online as it'll keep for ages and it takes rice to the next level.

*OK, it's not quite chicken, but it would have been lonely if it had its own section of the book.

### Ingredients

- 1 carrot, grated
- 1 red pepper, ½cm slices
- 2 spring onions, ½cm discs
- 250g skinless turkey breast, 1cm strips
- 1 chicken stock pot
- 150g white basmati rice
- 2 tbsp tomato ketchup
- 1 tbsp soy sauce
- 1 tbsp honey
- 1½ tbsp ketjap manis
- 1 lime
- flavourless oil
- 120g sugarsnap peas
- 30g coconut milk powder (optional)
- salt and black pepper

### Here's how...

**1** Put the kettle on to boil. Prep the **carrot, red pepper** and **spring onions**. On a separate chopping board, slice the **turkey** into 1cm wide strips.

**2** Dissolve the **chicken stock pot** in the boiling water in a large saucepan. Add the **rice** and put on a lid. Cook over a medium heat for 10 mins, then remove the pan from the heat and leave for another 10 mins. Do not touch the lid until 20 mins are up.

**3** In a small bowl, mix the **ketchup** with the **soy sauce, honey** and **ketjap manis**. Halve the **lime** and squeeze in the **juice** of one half. Cut the other half into wedges.

**4** Put 1 tbsp **oil** in a frying pan (or wok) over a high heat. When the **oil** is hot, stir-fry the **turkey** until browned on the outside, 5 mins. Add the **pepper** and cook for another 5 mins. Add the **sugarsnaps** and the **carrot**. Stir-fry for 3–4 mins, then add the **sauce**. Cook until bubbling and remove from the heat, checking that the **turkey** is cooked through and no longer pink in the middle.

**5** Jazz up your **rice** by stirring through half the **spring onions** and if you have any **coconut milk powder** then you can add that now too. Taste and add **salt** and **black pepper** if necessary.

**6** Spoon the **rice** into bowls and top with the **stir-fry**. Finish with a sprinkle of the remaining **spring onions**. Serve with **lime wedges** on the side for people to squeeze over as they please.

# FISH
## -&-
# SEAFOOD

# PRAWN & PROSCIUTTO LINGUINE

**READY IN 30 MINS**  **SERVES** (2)

All hail one of the most popular dishes ever to leave the HelloFresh Kitchen! This recipe is the stuff of legend and it's been making reappearances on our menu since we started. Why Ozone? In honour of the coffee shop around the corner from my house, where I'd sit at the bar and write our recipes. One day I got chatting to their Australian chef and he inspired me to make this super-quick summertime surf and turf. On the table in the time it takes to boil the pasta, but with the taste and looks of an Italian eatery in Capri. Beautiful.

## *Ingredients*

- **2 garlic cloves,** finely chopped
- **½ green chilli,** finely chopped
- **2 tbsp fresh chives,** finely chopped or snipped
- **6 slices prosciutto (or serrano ham),** 2cm widthway slices
- **150g raw tiger prawns,** chopped into 3 pieces
- **200g linguine**
- **1 vegetable stock pot**
- **olive oil**
- **3 tbsp crème fraîche**
- **½ lemon**
- **salt and black pepper**

## *Here's how...*

**1** Put a large pan of water over a high heat and bring to the boil. Prep the **garlic**, **chilli** and finely chop the **chives**. Roughly chop the **prosciutto** and the **prawns**. **Tip: It's even quicker to cut the prosciutto and chives with sharp scissors.**

**2** Once the water has come to the boil, add the **linguine** together with the **vegetable stock pot**. Don't discard the **stock** when the **linguine** is cooked as it's needed later for the sauce. Cook it for around 10 mins or until it is 'al dente' (cooked through but with a tiny bit of firmness left in the middle).

**3** Heat 1½ tbsp **olive oil** in a frying pan over a medium–high heat. Cook your **chilli**, **prosciutto** and **prawns** for 2 mins. Season with ¼ tsp **salt** and a few grinds of **black pepper**.

**4** When your **prawns** have just turned pink, add your **garlic**. Continue to cook for 1 min before adding in 4 tbsp of the **stock** from your pasta pan. Turn the heat to low and add the **crème fraîche** and three-quarters of your **chives**. Let your **sauce** simmer for a few mins until it goes thick and velvety. If the **sauce** still seems too thick, add another splash of **stock** water.

**5** Drain your **pasta** and add it to your **sauce**. Squeeze over 1 tbsp **lemon juice** and add a little more **salt** and **black pepper** if necessary. Toss the pan (or gently stir with a wooden spoon) to combine all of your ingredients.

**6** Serve with a sprinkle of your remaining **chives** and tuck in. Optional refreshments: Crack open a bottle of Prosecco (or Ribena if it's a school night).

# HERB-CRUSTED HADDOCK
## – WITH BITE-SIZED ROASTIES –

⏱ **READY IN 45 MINS**                    **SERVES** ②

There's a time and a place for fish fingers. It's usually a Sunday afternoon, sandwiched between some buttered bread with a healthy dollop of ketchup. But for all the other times there's this recipe. Equally easy (just about) but with a lot more cheffy kudos.

*Ingredients*

- **500g new potatoes**, bite-sized pieces
- **1½ tsp thyme leaves**, roughly chopped
- **olive oil**
- **1 leek**, 1cm dice
- **1 courgette**, 1cm dice
- **1 garlic clove**, finely chopped
- **1 tbsp butter**
- **2 haddock fillets**, about 150g each
- **100ml crème fraîche**
- **40g Parmesan**
- **20g panko breadcrumbs**
- **½ lemon**, or more to taste
- **salt and black pepper**

## *Here's how...*

**1** Preheat your oven to 220°C/Gas Mark 7. Wash and chop the **potatoes** into bite-sized pieces (no need to peel). Strip the **thyme leaves** from their stalks and roughly chop. Toss the **potatoes** in 1 tbsp **olive oil**, ½ tsp **salt** and half the **thyme leaves** (discard the stalks). Lay them flat on a baking tray and roast on the top shelf for around 25–30 mins, or until a little crispy at the edges.

**2** While the **potatoes** roast, get the rest of your prep done. Remove the root and green tops from the **leek**. Quarter it lengthways then chop into 1cm dice. Remove the top and bottom from the **courgette**. Quarter the **courgette** lengthways and then chop into 1cm dice also. Prep the **garlic**.

**3** Put the **butter** in a saucepan over a medium heat and add the **leek** and **courgette**. Cook for 8–10 mins or until soft. Stir frequently to make sure it doesn't brown.

**4** Coat each **haddock fillet** lightly in ½ tsp **olive oil** and season with ¼ tsp **salt** and a few grinds of **black pepper** on each side. Place on a baking tray and spread 1 tsp **crème fraîche** onto the flesh side of each fillet. Mix the **Parmesan** with the remaining **thyme**, **panko breadcrumbs** and 1 tbsp **olive oil** in a small bowl. Grate in the **lemon zest** (more if you like) and mix well. Sprinkle the crumb over the **crème fraîche** and pat down gently to make sure the mixture sticks to the **haddock**.

**5** Bake the **haddock** on the top shelf of your preheated oven for 10–12 mins, until the crust is golden brown and the fish is cooked through. Meanwhile return to the veggies. Add the **garlic** to the pan. Cook for 1 min. Season with ¼ tsp **salt** and a few grinds of **black pepper** and then add the remaining **crème fraîche**. Reduce the heat to low and gently bring the sauce to a simmer. Cut the **lemon** into wedges.

**6** When the fish is golden, spoon the creamy **leeks** into the centre of your plates. Surround with the **roasted potatoes** and then carefully place the **herb-crusted haddock** on top. Serve with a wedge of **lemon**.

# COASTAL FISH CURRY

🌓 **READY IN 35 MINS**  **SERVES** ②

This popular little number hails from Mimi's gap 'yah' (phonetic spelling). She was travelling around India and had a curry like this on a beautiful beach called Varkala. They served theirs on a banana leaf and Mimi says yours would be all the better for it too.

## *Ingredients*

- ½ **lime**, zest and juice
- 2 **tilapia** (or other chunky white fish, like cod) **fillets**, about 150g each
- 1 **vegetable stock pot**
- 2 **cardamom pods**, crushed
- 150g **basmati rice**
- 1 **onion**, 1cm dice
- 1 **garlic clove**, finely chopped
- 2 tbsp **fresh coriander**, roughly chopped
- 150g **green beans**, trimmed and chopped into three pieces
- **flavourless oil**
- 1 tsp **mustard seeds**
- 1½ tsp **Sri Lankan curry powder**\*
- 400ml **coconut milk**
- **salt** and **black pepper**

## *Here's how...*

**1** Zest and juice the **lime**. Put the **juice** in a mixing bowl and set the **zest** aside for later. Cut each **tilapia fillet** into four pieces and add to the bowl. Season with ¼ tsp **salt** and a few grinds of **black pepper**. Set aside to marinate.

**2** Put 300ml water for the **rice** in a large saucepan with half the **vegetable stock pot**. Whack the **cardamom pods** on your chopping board with the bottom of a saucepan to crack them open, then add to the pan. Bring to a boil, stir to dissolve the **stock pot** and add the **rice**. Reduce to a medium heat, put on a lid and cook for 10 mins. Then remove from the heat and set aside for another 10 mins. For perfectly cooked **rice** don't peek under the lid until 20 mins are up.

**3** Prep the **onion**, **garlic** and **coriander**. Trim the ends from the **green beans** and discard, then chop the **green beans** into three pieces.

**4** Put 1 tbsp **oil** in a frying pan over a medium heat and add the **mustard seeds**. Keep an eye on them as if you leave them for too long they'll start jumping out of the pan. Once they begin to pop, add the **onion** and **lime zest**. Cook over a low heat until the **onion is soft**, 5 mins, then add the **Sri Lankan curry powder** and **garlic**. Cook for 1 min more.

**5** Pour the **coconut milk** into your pan. Add the remaining **vegetable stock pot** and the **green beans**. Stir everything together. Simmer gently for 2–3 mins.

**6** Carefully add the **fish** along with any **lime juice** left in the bowl. Gently submerge it in the sauce but be careful not to break the pieces up. Put a lid on the pan and poach the **fish** over a low heat for 4 mins. Remove the **cardamom** pieces from the **rice** and fluff it up with a fork. Serve your delicious **fish curry** atop a generous heap of **rice** with the chopped **coriander** for good measure.

## Hello
## SPICE

*You can easily get Sri Lankan curry powder online from seasonedpioneers.com but failing that, use a regular curry powder.

# SIMPLY SIMON'S SUMPTUOUS SEA BASS
## – WITH THAI TOMATOES –

**READY IN 35 MINS**  **SERVES** (2)

Back in the day, whenever we needed a bit of extra inspiration in the HelloFresh Kitchen, we'd launch a little office cooking competition. This dish was inspired by one of our interns, Simon, and it's been on the menu ever since. Don't be put off by the strong scent of fish sauce, Thailand's favourite seasoning: once it's mixed into a sauce, it loses that strength and adds an incredible hit of salty umami-ness.

*Ingredients*

- 2 garlic cloves, finely chopped
- 1 onion, ½cm dice
- 1 tsp fresh ginger, peeled and finely chopped
- 350g new potatoes, halved
- olive oil
- 2 vine tomatoes, peeled and cut into ½cm dice
- 3 tbsp fresh coriander, roughly chopped
- 2 sea bass fillets, about 100g each
- 2 tsp butter
- ½ lime
- 1 tbsp fish sauce
- salt and black pepper

*Here's how...*

**1** Preheat your oven to 220°C/Gas Mark 7. Put a medium pan of water over a high heat and bring to the boil. Prep the **garlic**, **onion** and **ginger**. Cut the **potatoes** in half (no need to peel).

**2** Toss the **potatoes** in 1 tbsp **olive oil**, ½ tsp **salt** and a few grinds of **black pepper**. Lay them flat on a baking tray and roast on the top shelf for around 25 mins, or until a little crispy at the edges.

**3** Slice just through the skin of each **tomato** from the top to the bottom. Repeat three more times around each **tomato** so that the skin is sliced into four segments. Place the **tomatoes** in the boiling water for 60 seconds.

**4** Run the **tomatoes** under cold water to cool them down, then peel off their skin (the segmenting makes this easier). Chop the **tomatoes** into ½cm dice.

**5** Heat 1 tbsp **olive oil** in a frying pan over a medium–low heat. Add the **garlic** and **onion** and cook for 5 mins, until soft. Add the **tomatoes**, turn the heat to low and bubble away for 15 mins. Add 1 tbsp water now and again if the ingredients start to dry out. Meanwhile, prep the **coriander**.

**6** Heat 1 tbsp **olive oil** in another frying pan over a medium–high heat. Sprinkle a bit of **salt** (less than ¼ tsp) onto both sides of the **sea bass** and place in the pan skin side-down. Cook for 2 mins until the skin has crisped up then gently turn over. Add the **butter** and a squeeze of **lime** to the pan then remove the fish from the heat. The **fish** will carry on cooking off the heat.

**7** Add the **ginger** and 2 tbsp chopped **coriander** to the **tomatoes**, then add the **fish sauce** bit by bit and taste as you go along as it's quite strong. Serve the fish on a bed of the **crispy potatoes** and **sauce** with the remaining chopped **coriander** sprinkled over and something cold and refreshing on the side.

# PAN-FRIED SEA BREAM
## – WITH SAFFRON MASH –

🕐 **READY IN 40 MINS**     **SERVES** ②

Some nights you want to keep things low key and simple. Other nights you want to get a little more jazzy (though not at the expense of that simplicity). This recipe is for the latter. Saffron is definitely at the more luxurious end of the spice spectrum, but you'll only be using the smallest amount by infusing its flavour and beautiful colour in a little bit of milk for your mash. A perfect dinner for an impromptu celebration or forgotten anniversary.

*Ingredients*

- 500g potatoes, 2cm dice
- 2 tbsp milk
- a pinch of saffron*
- 220g cherry tomatoes (mix of red and yellow if possible), halved lengthways
- 3 tbsp fresh basil, roughly chopped
- ½ lemon
- olive oil
- 60g chorizo, 1cm dice
- 150ml crème fraîche
- 200g sugarsnap peas
- 2 sea bream fillets, about 150g each
- salt and black pepper

*Here's how...*

**1** Put a large pan of water with ½ tsp **salt** over a high heat and bring to the boil. Peel the **potatoes** and roughly chop into 2cm dice. Once the water has come to the boil, add the **potatoes** and cook until you can easily slip a knife through them, 15–20 mins.

**2** Heat the **milk** (for such a small amount you can do it in a cup in the microwave) until it's just steaming, then add in your **saffron**, give it a swirl and leave it aside for later.

**3** Meanwhile, cut the **cherry tomatoes** in half lengthways. Pull the **basil leaves** off their **stalks**. Finely chop the **stalks** and roughly chop the **leaves**, keeping the **stalks** and **leaves** separate. Squeeze the **lemon juice** into a bowl, add the **tomatoes**, **basil leaves** and a few grinds of **black pepper** and mix together.

**4** Heat 1 tbsp **olive oil** in a large frying pan over a medium heat. Chop your **chorizo** into 1cm dice, add to the frying pan and cook, stirring occasionally, until it's slightly crisp and has released some of its delicious oil, 3–4 mins. Transfer the cooked **chorizo** and its cooking oil to your **tomato** bowl and stir gently to combine. Reserve the pan to cook your fish later. Put another pan of water over a high heat and bring to the boil for the **sugarsnap peas**.

**5** Once the **potatoes** are soft, drain them and then pop them back into your pan. Mash until smooth and then stir in the **basil stalks**, the **saffron milk**, **crème fraîche**, ½ tsp **salt** and a few grinds of **black pepper**. Taste and add more seasoning if you think it needs it. Pop the lid on and leave to the side to keep warm.

**6** Add the **sugarsnap peas** to the boiling water to cook for 4 mins. Once cooked, drain.

**7** Meanwhile, heat 1 tbsp **olive oil** in a frying pan over a medium–high heat. Season each side of the **sea bream** with ¼ tsp **salt** and a few grinds of **black pepper**. Lay the **sea bream fillets** in your frying pan skin-side down and cook for 3 mins (don't move them while they're cooking), then turn and cook for 2 mins on the other side, until the **fish** is cooked and white all the way through. Remove from the heat. To serve, add a spoonful of **potatoes** to each plate, then add your **sea bream** and **sugarsnaps** and top with the **tomato salsa**.

## Hello
## PINCH?!

*We've religiously avoided
using the vague term 'pinch of'
in this book but here you quite
literally only need the amount
of saffron you can pinch
between your thumb and your
index finger. A little goes
a long way.

# MOROCCAN-SPICED SALMON

## – WITH LEMON & CARAMELISED ONION COUSCOUS –

**READY IN 35 MINS**          **SERVES** ②

We're always on the hunt for new tips and tricks to shortcut the cooking process. Peeling ginger with a spoon and grating garlic instead of chopping are up there amongst the most popular. But couscous is another. If you want to whip up dinner in no time at all then it's one of the easiest accompaniments out there. So much so that you can even make it at work using a bowl and a kettle. For videos of our latest hacks check out our Facebook page by searching HelloFreshUK.

### Ingredients

- 1 tbsp ras-el-hanout spice
- olive oil
- 2 salmon fillets, about 150g each
- ½ red onion, ½cm dice
- 2 tbsp fresh mint leaves, finely chopped
- 2 vine tomatoes, ½cm dice
- ½ lemon, zest and juice
- ½ vegetable stock cube
- 150g couscous
- 2 tbsp butter
- salt and black pepper

### Here's how...

**1** Mix the **ras-el-hanout** (add less if you want less heat) in a small bowl with 1 tbsp **olive oil**. Rub the mixture all over the **salmon** and season with ¼ tsp **salt** and a few grinds of **black pepper**. Leave to the side to marinate while you prep everything else.

**2** Prep the **onion**. Heat 1½ tbsp **olive oil** in a saucepan over a low heat. Add the **onion** with ¼ tsp **salt** and a few grinds of **black pepper**. Cook slowly with a lid on the pan until very soft, 15–20 mins. Check regularly to make sure it's not sticking to the pan. If it does, turn down the heat and add a dash of water.

**3** While the **onion** cooks, finely chop the **mint leaves** and discard the stalks. Chop the **vine tomatoes** into ½cm dice. Zest ½ tsp **lemon zest** and then halve the **lemon** widthways, ready to juice.

**4** Once the **onion** is soft, add 300ml water to the pan. Bring to the boil, add the **vegetable stock cube** and stir to dissolve. Remove the pan from the heat. Add the **couscous** and stir everything together. Place a lid on the pan and leave to the side for 10 mins whilst you cook the **salmon**.

**5** Preheat your grill to high. Heat 1 tbsp **olive oil** in a frying pan over a medium heat. Once hot, place the **salmon** in the pan skin-side down. Cook for 4 mins without moving the **salmon**. Then place the pan under your grill. Grill the **salmon** for 4–5 mins until cooked and opaque all the way through. Remove from under your grill and return the pan to a medium heat. Add the **butter** to the pan and squeeze over 1 tbsp **lemon juice**. Spoon the **juice** over the **salmon** then take off the heat.

**6** Stir the **mint** and **tomato** into the **couscous** along with ¼ tsp **lemon zest** (add more if you want it really citrussy). Pour any juices from the pan into the **couscous** and stir. To serve, place the **couscous** into bowls, top it off with the **salmon** and squeeze over a little more **lemon juice**.

# KING PRAWN LINGUINE
## – WITH CHILLI & SUN-DRIED TOMATO –

**READY IN 20 MINS**
(depending on your chopping speed)

**SERVES** (2)

Sometimes even 30 minutes of cooking in the evening is too much to face. That's when the cereal cupboard gets opened. With your chopping skills up to scratch (having studiously worked through the Cooking Tips at the start of this book), you should be able to have this one on the table in the time it takes to cook the pasta. On your marks…

### Ingredients

- 1 onion, ½cm dice
- 2 garlic cloves, finely chopped
- 2 tbsp sun-dried tomatoes, finely chopped
- ½ mild red chilli, deseeded and finely chopped
- 3 tbsp fresh flat leaf parsley, finely chopped
- 250g raw king prawns, halved lengthways
- olive oil
- 200g linguine
- 1 tbsp red wine vinegar
- 1 tin chopped tomatoes
- 200ml tomato passata
- ¼ tsp sugar
- salt and black pepper

### Here's how…

**1** Put a large saucepan of water with 1 tbsp **salt** over a high heat and bring to the boil for the pasta. Prep the **onion, garlic, sun-dried tomatoes** and **red chilli**. Pick the **parsley leaves** from their **stalks** and finely chop both (keeping them separate). Lastly, cut the **prawns** in half lengthways.

**2** Heat 1½ tbsp **oil** in a frying pan over a medium heat. Once hot, add the **onion, garlic, sun-dried tomatoes** and as much **chilli** as you dare. Season with ¼ tsp **salt** and a grind of **black pepper**. Cook until the **onion** is soft, about 5 mins.

**3** Add the **linguine** to your pan of boiling water. Cook until 'al dente' (cooked through but with a tiny bit of firmness left in the middle), about 11 mins (or according to the packet instructions). Once cooked, drain the **linguine** in a colander.

**4** Add the **red wine vinegar**, the tin of **chopped tomatoes** and **passata**, **parsley stalks** and **sugar**. Let the mixture simmer over a medium–low heat until you have a nice thick **sauce**, about 10 mins.

**5** Once the **sauce** has thickened, stir in the **king prawns**. Cook for 2–3 mins until the **prawns** are pink on the outside and opaque all the way through.

**6** Combine the **pasta** and **sauce**. Sprinkle over most of the **parsley leaves** and toss everything together to mix thoroughly. Serve sprinkled with the remaining **parsley leaves**.

# PAN-FRIED SEA BASS
## – WITH VIBRANT SALSA VERDE & MINI ROASTIES –

🕐 **READY IN 30 MINS**　　　　　　　**SERVES** ②

We've always made a point of avoiding the old-fashioned jargon that makes cooking a lot more intimidating and mysterious than it should be. That said, sometimes a bit of romance language goes a long way. So in this instance we're sticking to salsa verde rather than 'green sauce'.

### *Ingredients*

- **350g new potatoes,** halved lengthways
- **olive oil**
- **1 garlic clove,** finely chopped
- **1 tbsp capers,** very finely chopped
- **30g pitted green olives,** very finely chopped
- **3 tbsp fresh flat leaf parsley,** finely chopped
- **3 tbsp fresh mint leaves,** finely chopped
- **1 lemon,** zest and juice
- **150g green beans,** trimmed
- **2 sea bass fillets,** about 100g each
- **salt and black pepper**

### *Here's how...*

**1** Preheat your oven to 220°C/Gas Mark 7. Wash and chop the **potatoes** in half lengthways (no need to peel). Toss in 1 tbsp **olive oil**, ½ tsp **salt** and a grind of **black pepper**. Lay them flat on a baking tray and roast on the top shelf for around 25 mins, or until a little crispy at the edges.

**2** Prep the **garlic**. Very, very finely chop the **capers** and **olives**. Finely chop the **parsley** (stalks and all) and the **mint leaves** (no stalks).

**3** Mix your chopped **parsley** and **mint** with your chopped **olives, garlic** and **capers**. Roll the **lemon** firmly under the heel of your hand on the chopping board to loosen up its juices. Zest in the **zest** from the whole **lemon** and then cut it in half and squeeze in all of its **juice** together with 3 tbsp **olive oil**. Whisk together thoroughly using a fork and leave to the side.

**4** Bring a pan of water to the boil with ½ tsp **salt**. Trim the ends from the **green beans** and discard the ends. Add the **green beans** to the boiling water and cook for 2 mins, then drain and run cold water through them to stop them cooking any more.

**5** About 6 mins before the **potatoes** are cooked, add 1 tbsp **olive oil** to a frying pan over a medium heat. Season both sides of each **sea bass fillet** with ¼ tsp **salt** and a good grind of **black pepper** and, once the pan is hot, add the **sea bass** skin-side down. Cook for 3 mins on one side before turning over to cook for 2 mins on the other side.

**6** Gently mix your **green beans** and **potatoes** together and serve a pile in the middle of each plate. Lay your **sea bass** over the top and finish with a big spoonful of your beautiful, vibrant **salsa verde**.

# SRI LANKAN PRAWN PILAF

## – WITH BEETROOT & HERB SLAW –

🕐 **READY IN 40 MINS**  **SERVES** (2)

Cooking something new is a bit like taking an alternative route to work in the morning. There's that pressure that you need to get to your final destination, mingled with the uncertainty whether this new direction will even get you there. But of course the upside is making a new discovery that adds a bit of variety to your life. Fortunately Chef André has been scouting ahead for this recipe and guarantees that the route is both quicker and more delicious than your usual dinner-time commute.

*You can easily get this online from seasonedpioneers.com but failing that, use a regular curry powder.

### Ingredients

- ½ onion, ½cm dice
- 1 courgette, 1cm dice
- 1 garlic clove, finely chopped
- 1 vegetable stock pot
- olive oil
- 1 tbsp curry powder (Sri Lankan mix if possible)*
- 150g white basmati rice
- 1 lemon, zest and juice
- 3 tbsp fresh flat leaf parsley, roughly chopped
- 250g raw king prawns
- 1 beetroot
- salt and black pepper

### Here's how...

**1** Boil a kettle of water. Prep the **onion, courgette** and **garlic**. Once the kettle has boiled, pour 300ml water into a measuring jug with the **vegetable stock pot** and stir to dissolve.

**2** Put 1½ tbsp **olive oil** in a large saucepan over a medium heat. Add the **onion** and cook until soft, around 6 mins. Stir in the **garlic** and **curry powder**. Cook for 1 min more, then add the **basmati rice** and stir. Add the **courgette** and stock. Bring to the boil then put on a lid. Simmer for 10 mins over a medium heat, then remove from the heat and set aside for another 10 mins. Don't peek under the lid until 20 mins are up or the **rice** won't cook perfectly.

**3** Zest the **lemon** and roughly chop the **parsley** (stalks and all). Put half the **parsley** in a mixing bowl and add half the **lemon zest** and 1½ tbsp **olive oil**. Roll the **lemon** firmly under the heel of your hand on the chopping board to loosen up its juices and then cut it in half and squeeze the **juice** of one half into the mixing bowl.

**4** Put 1 tbsp **oil** in a frying pan over a medium heat. When hot, add the **prawns**. Season with ¼ tsp **salt**, a few grinds of **black pepper** and ½ tbsp **lemon juice** and cook, stirring occasionally, for 5 mins, until the **prawns** are pink on the outside and opaque all the way through.

**5** Peel and coarsely grate the **beetroot** and add it to the bowl with the **parsley dressing**. Season with ¼ tsp **salt** and a few grinds of **black pepper**. Taste and add more **salt, pepper, lemon juice** or **zest** as you desire. Check that the **prawns** are cooked and give them a bit longer if needed.

**6** Stir the **prawns** into the **pilaf**, squeeze in 1 tbsp **lemon juice** and add the remaining **parsley**. Taste the **pilaf** and season with **salt, black pepper** or more **lemon** if you like. Serve a generous amount for each person – making sure the **prawns** are evenly distributed – and add some **beetroot slaw** on the side.

# GRILLED SALMON TARATOR
## – WITH BULGUR WHEAT TABBOULEH –

🌗 **READY IN 35 MINS**  **SERVES** ② 

You might be wondering what a tarator is. We all did when Chef André brought it around for taste testing. He explained that it's a lovely yoghurt-based sauce from Bulgaria. We've used crème fraîche here for a richer taste so it's perfect with warm salmon fillets and herby bulgur wheat.

*Ingredients*

- 1 vegetable stock pot
- 100g cracked bulgur wheat
- 2 salmon fillets, about 150g each
- olive oil
- 1 red onion, thin half moons
- 1 tbsp red wine vinegar
- 1 garlic clove, finely chopped
- ½ cucumber, half moons
- 3 tbsp fresh mint, finely chopped
- 3 tbsp fresh flat leaf parsley, finely chopped
- 3 tbsp fresh coriander, finely chopped
- 1 lemon, zest and juice
- 1½ tsp tahini
- 150ml crème fraîche
- 4 tbsp walnuts, crushed
- 1 red chilli, finely chopped
- salt and black pepper

*Here's how...*

**1** Preheat your grill to a medium heat.

**2** Put a saucepan of 200ml water over a medium heat with the **stock pot** and stir to dissolve. Add the **bulgur wheat** and bring to the boil. When boiling, cover with a lid, take off the heat and leave to rest for 15 mins.

**3** Meanwhile, rub each **salmon fillet** with 1 tsp **olive oil**, ¼ tsp **salt** and a grind of **black pepper**. Lay them on a foil-lined baking tray, skin-side down. Grill for 10–12 mins, until the the centre is opaque and cooked through. Once cooked, allow the **salmon** to cool – we'll be serving it warm, not hot.

**4** Slice the **onion** as thinly as you can. Put 1½ tbsp **oil** in a frying pan over a medium heat. Add the **onion**. Cook stirring frequently until soft, about 7 mins. Season with ¼ tsp **salt**, then add the **red wine vinegar**. Allow it to evaporate completely, then remove the pan from the heat and set aside.

**5** Prep the **garlic**. Cut the **cucumber** in half lengthways, scoop out the seeds (you can use the tip of a teaspoon) and discard. Slice the **cucumber** into half moons. Pick the **mint**, **parsley** and **coriander leaves** from their stalks and roughly chop (discard the stalks). Roll the **lemon** firmly under the heel of your hand on the chopping board to loosen up its juices and then zest and juice it. Mix the **garlic** and **tahini** into the **crème fraîche** with half the **mint**, **parsley** and **coriander**, ½ tsp **lemon zest** and half the **lemon juice**. Taste and add a bit more **salt** and **black pepper** if you need. Pop the **walnuts** in a freezer bag and whack them with a wooden spoon to break them up into pieces. Chop the **red chilli** as finely as you can.

**6** When the **bulgur wheat** is ready, stir through 1 tbsp **olive oil** along with the **cucumber**, remaining chopped herbs, 1 tsp **lemon zest** and 2 tbsp **lemon juice**. Check the seasoning and add a little more **salt** if necessary. Spread a generous amount of the **crème fraîche** mixture on the flesh-side of each **salmon fillet** so it is completely coated. Top with the **walnuts** and a sprinkle of **red chilli**.

**7** Serve the **bulgur wheat** in bowls, spread the **red onion** on top and finish with the **salmon tarator**.

# GARLICKY PRAWNS

## – WITH PROPER MINI ROAST POTATOES & WALNUT PARSLEY PESTO –

🕐 **READY IN 40 MINS**  SERVES ②

One of the wizards behind the HelloFresh curtain is Ellie, who sends customer recommendations to the chefs for future creations. In moments of culinary abandon she'll also allow a wild card recipe where we can pair together whatever we want. For Mimi this was another chance to put her favourite food front and centre: The Roast Potato. She even claims it's the best roast potato in this book. We'll let you be the judge of that.

### *Ingredients*

- **500g potatoes**, peeled and chopped into 3cm dice
- **olive oil**
- **3 tbsp fresh flat leaf parsley**, finely chopped
- **40g Parmesan**, grated
- **3 tbsp walnuts**, crushed
- **1 red onion**, 1cm dice
- **1 garlic clove**, finely chopped
- **250g cherry tomatoes**, halved lengthways
- **250g raw king** or **tiger prawns**
- **40g rocket leaves**
- **salt and black pepper**

### *Here's how...*

**1** Preheat your oven to 220°/Gas Mark 7. Put a large saucepan of water with 1 tsp salt over a high heat and bring to the boil. Peel the **potatoes**, chop into 3cm dice, and add to your pan of boiling water. Boil the **potatoes** for 5 mins, then drain in a colander. Meanwhile, pour 1½ tbsp **olive oil** onto a baking tray and put it on the top shelf of your oven. This helps make your **potatoes** super crispy.

**2** Give the **potatoes** a good shake in your colander to fluff up their edges and create a greater surface area for crisping. Gently tip the **potatoes** onto your hot baking tray – be careful not to burn yourself. Spread out in an even layer and season with ¼ tsp **salt**. Roast on the top shelf of your oven until crisp and golden, around 25 mins. Turn halfway through cooking.

**3** Meanwhile, prep the **parsley** and **Parmesan**. Pop the **walnuts** in a freezer bag and whack them with a wooden spoon to break them up into pieces. Put the chopped **parsley**, **walnuts** and **Parmesan** in a bowl and add 5 tbsp **olive oil** (use 7 tbsp if you are making it for four people, rather than the usual technique of doubling ingredients). Season with ¼ tsp **salt** and a few grinds of **black pepper**, mix well and set aside.

**4** Prep the **onion** and **garlic** and cut the **cherry tomatoes** in half lengthways. Heat 1½ tbsp **olive oil** in a frying pan over a medium heat and add the **onion**. Cook until soft and slightly brown, 10 mins. If the **onion** is browning too much, just turn the heat down a little.

**5** When the **onion** is cooked, add the **tomatoes**, **garlic** and **prawns**. Season with ¼ tsp **salt** and a few grinds of **black pepper**. Cook for 4–5 mins, or until the **tomatoes** are slightly soft and the **prawns** are cooked (pink on the outside and opaque all the way through). Once cooked, remove the pan from the heat.

**6** Divide the **mini roast potatoes** between plates. Put a handful of **rocket** on top and a generous portion of **prawns** on top of that. Finish by drizzling over the **walnutty pesto** to serve.

# ROASTED SALMON

## – WITH GARLICKY TOMATOES & CRUSHED POTATOES –

**READY IN 25 MINS**     **SERVES** (2)

If you're anything like us, then the sight of 16 ingredients in a recipe is definitely not welcome when you get home from a busy day at 8pm. This little number was designed with minimum mid-week intimidation and maximum flavour in mind. We've also squeezed in reusing your pot of water and frying pan for extra speed. 3, 2, 1, go!

### Ingredients

- 2 garlic cloves, finely sliced
- 3 tbsp fresh flat leaf parsley, roughly chopped
- 150g green beans, trimmed
- 250g cherry tomatoes, halved lengthways
- 450g new potatoes, halved
- 2 salmon fillets, about 150g each
- olive oil
- 2 tsp butter
- salt and black pepper

## Here's how...

**1** Preheat your oven to 200°C/Gas Mark 6. Put a pot of water over a high heat with 1 tsp **salt** and bring to the boil. Prep the **garlic** and **parsley**. Trim the ends off the **green beans** and discard the ends. Cut the **cherry tomatoes** in half lengthways.

**2** 'Blanch' your **green beans** by adding them to the boiling water for 2 mins, then remove them from the pot (you can use a slotted spoon for this) and put them in a bowl of cold water. **Tip: Keep the boiling water to save time and pans.** Chop the **potatoes** in half and quarter any big ones. Add your **potatoes** to the boiling water that your beans were in and cook for 15–20 mins. Your **potatoes** are cooked when you can easily slip a knife through them.

**3** Meanwhile, drizzle each **salmon fillet** with 1 tsp **olive oil** and season with ¼ tsp **salt** and a few grinds of **black pepper** on each side. Place on a baking tray, skin-side down and roast for 8–10 mins, until the **fish** easily flakes with a fork.

**4** When the **potatoes** are cooked, drain them and set aside. Meanwhile, melt the **butter** in a frying pan over a medium heat. Add your **tomatoes** and season with ¼ tsp **salt** and a few grinds of **black pepper**. Cook for about 2 mins, until slightly burst. Drain your **green beans** and then add them to the pan to cook, tossing regularly, for a few mins. Add your **garlic** and half the **parsley** and cook for 30 seconds, until fragrant. Set aside on a plate.

**5** Once your **potatoes** are done, crush them slightly with a fork. In the same pan you cooked the **tomatoes** in, heat 2 tsp **olive oil** over a medium heat. Add your **potatoes** and cook for about 3 mins on each side, until golden brown and crispy. Sprinkle with your remaining **parsley** and season with ¼ tsp **salt** and a few grinds of **black pepper**.

**6** Serve your **salmon fillets** with your **green beans, tomatoes** and **crispy potatoes**.

# CAJUN COD

## – WITH ROASTED SWEET POTATOES & AVOCADO CREAM –

🕐 **READY IN 35 MINS**   **SERVES** ②

'Fusion food' existed a long time before trendy restaurants started using the phrase. Way back in the 18th century, French, Spanish and African settlers all congregated in America's Deep South. They pooled their culinary heritage and Cajun food was born. This beautiful little combination is a favourite of Chef André, who says a glass of cold Riesling wouldn't go amiss with it either.

*Ingredients*

- 600g **sweet potato**, 2cm dice
- **olive oil**
- 220g **cherry tomatoes** (mix of red and yellow if possible), halved lengthways
- 1 **lime**, zest and juice
- 3 tbsp fresh **coriander**, finely chopped
- 1 **avocado**, roughly chopped
- 150g **soured cream**
- 1 tbsp **plain flour**
- 1½ tsp **Cajun spice mix**
- 2 **cod fillets**, about 175g each
- 60g **rocket leaves**
- **salt** and **black pepper**

*Here's how...*

**1** Preheat your oven to 200°C/Gas Mark 6. Cut the **sweet potato** into 2cm dice (no need to peel). Put on a baking tray and drizzle over 1½ tbsp **olive oil**. Season with ½ tsp **salt** and and a few grinds of **black pepper**. Mix to coat the **potato** evenly, then roast in the oven until soft and browned at the edges, 20–25 mins. Turn halfway through cooking.

**2** Cut the **cherry tomatoes** in half lengthways and put them in a bowl. Season with ¼ tsp **salt**. **Tip: The salt will draw the juices out of the tomatoes and create a delicious base for the dressing.** Grate in the zest of half the **lime** and add 1 tbsp **olive oil**. Roughly chop the **coriander** and add two-thirds to the **tomatoes**. Stir, cover and set aside.

**3** Halve the **avocado** lengthways and twist apart. Remove the stone and slip a dinner knife around the edge of the flesh to pop the flesh out of its skin. Chop half into small dice and put in a small bowl. Mash to a smooth paste with a fork and add a squeeze of **lime juice** and ¼ tsp **salt**. Stir in the **soured cream** and mix until smooth.

**4** Chop the other half of the **avocado** into 2cm dice and toss it with the **tomatoes**.

**5** Put the **flour** in a mixing bowl with the **Cajun spice** and ¼ tsp **salt**. Add the **cod** to the bowl and coat it in the **flour mixture**. Put 1 tbsp **olive oil** in a frying pan over a medium–high heat. When hot, add the **fish** to the pan, skin-side down. Fry until golden, about 4 mins. Then turn and fry the other side, another 4 mins, until cooked and white all the way through.

**6** Share the **rocket** between your plates, covering the whole base of each, then nestle the **sweet potato dice** amongst the **leaves**. Pop the **cod** in the centre and then spoon the **tomatoes** and **juices** around and over the **fish**. Serve with a sprinkle of the remaining **coriander** and the **avocado cream** on the side.

# PAN-FRIED SALMON
## – IN A DILL & BUTTER SAUCE WITH ROCKET NEW POTATOES –

🌓 **READY IN 25 MINS**  **SERVES** ②

This one's a speedy recipe so I won't take up any more of your time telling a story…get cracking!

### Ingredients

- **450g new potatoes**, quartered
- **1 lemon**, zest and juice
- **½ tbsp fresh dill**, finely chopped
- **1 tsp capers**, finely chopped
- **2 salmon fillets**, about 150g each
- **olive oil**
- **2 tbsp butter**
- **50g rocket leaves**
- **salt and black pepper**

### Here's how...

**1** Put a pot of water with ½ tsp **salt** over a high heat and bring to the boil. Chop the **new potatoes** into quarters (no need to peel) and put them in the boiling water for around 10–12 mins, or until just soft enough to eat. Drain and keep to the side.

**2** Zest ½ tsp **lemon zest**, prep the **dill leaves** and **capers** and keep to the side for later. Season each **salmon fillet** on both sides with ¼ tsp **salt**, a few grinds of **black pepper** and preheat your grill to high.

**3** Put a frying pan over a medium–high heat with 1 tbsp **olive oil**. Once the pan is hot, lay in the **salmon**, skin-side down. Leave it to cook for around 4 mins and resist the temptation to move the **fish**, as it may stick to the pan.

**4** Remove the pan from the heat and put under the grill for around 5 mins with the handle facing outwards.

**5** After 5 mins, take the pan from under the grill using a tea towel or oven glove to touch the hot handle. Place the pan back on the hob and add 1 tbsp **butter**.

**6** Once the **butter** has melted and starts to foam, squeeze in the **juice** of the **lemon** and spoon these juices over the **salmon** before removing it to a plate.

**7** Add another 1 tbsp **butter** to the pan and cook until it foams and goes very slightly brown (they call this 'beurre noisette', but we call it foamy butter). Take the frying pan off the heat, scatter in the **dill**, half the **lemon zest** and the **capers** and season with ¼ tsp **salt** and some **black pepper**.

**8** Season the **new potatoes** with a bit of **salt** (less than ¼ tsp) and a few grinds of **black pepper**. Scatter over the remaining **lemon zest** for a burst of citrus flavour. Portion out the **potatoes**, scatter over the **rocket leaves**, place the **salmon** on top and pour over a bit of the **dill and caper sauce** to serve.

# HOT-SMOKED SALMON SPAGHETTI

🌗 **READY IN 30 MINS**                          **SERVES** ②

The word 'cheat' is subjective. To puritans, it can be any shortcut. These are people who will happily spend days bubbling down a stock to get it just right, or lovingly nurturing a sourdough starter as if it were their newborn. I have a genuine admiration for those people – they maintain the artisanal element of cooking that I find so magical. But let's be realistic: Wednesday at 8pm is not the time to get artisanal. That's what this little number is all about. Is hot-smoked salmon a cheat? I prefer the term 'life hack'.

## Ingredients

- 1 echalion shallot (the long one), ½cm dice
- 1 small bunch of fresh chives (about 10g), finely chopped or snipped
- ½ red chilli, finely chopped
- ½ head broccoli, florets separated and chopped
- 1 hot-smoked salmon fillet, about 180g
- 1 garlic clove, finely chopped
- 200g spaghetti
- olive oil
- 1 vegetable stock pot
- 100ml crème fraîche
- ½ lemon
- salt and black pepper

## Here's how...

**1** Put a saucepan of water with 1 tbsp **salt** over a high heat and bring to the boil. Prep the **shallot** and **chives**. Deseed and prep the **chilli**. Cut the **broccoli** into florets and slice each floret into four. Remove the skin from the **salmon** and put the flesh in a bowl. Use two forks to pull it apart into large flakes. Prep the **garlic**.

**2** Add the **spaghetti** to your pan of boiling water and cook until 'al dente' (cooked through but with a tiny bit of firmness left in the middle), 11 mins (or according to the packet instructions). Once done, reserve 150ml of the pasta water, drain the **spaghetti** in a colander and return to the pan (off the heat). Toss with 1 tbsp **olive oil** to stop it sticking together.

**3** While your pasta cooks, put a frying pan over a medium–high heat with 1 tbsp **olive oil**. Once hot, add the **broccoli**, ¼ tsp **salt** and a few grinds of **black pepper**. Cook until slightly brown and crispy, 7–8 mins, then remove from the pan.

**4** Add another tbsp **olive oil** to the pan (no need to wash it) and turn the heat down to medium. Add the **shallot** and cook until slightly softened, 4 mins. Then add the **garlic** and **chilli** (don't add it all if you prefer your food with less heat) and cook for 1 min more.

**5** Add the **vegetable stock pot** to the pan along with the reserved **pasta water**. Bring to the boil and stir to dissolve the **stock pot**. Simmer for 2 mins, then stir in the **crème fraîche**. Add ¼ tsp **salt**, a few grinds of **black pepper** and bring to a gentle simmer again. Lower the heat and simmer for another 2 mins.

**6** Squeeze in **lemon juice** to your taste, then add the **salmon**, **broccoli** and **chives** to the pan. Stir gently then take off the heat. Add the **spaghetti**, toss everything together and serve in bowls.

## Hello
## HOT-SMOKED SALMON

*These are the chunky fillets of salmon that have already been cooked by hot-smoking them. Not to be confused with slivers of smoked salmon.

# -RED-
# MEAT

# NICK 'THE KNIFE' STEAK
## – WITH ROSEMARY ROASTED SWEET POTATOES –

🕐 **READY IN 30 MINS**                    **SERVES** ②

When a recipe only has a handful of ingredients, each one has to be a total belter, so we've always searched out suppliers who can cut the mustard. That's why we starting working with Simon and his brother Nick 'The Knife' Mellin at Roaming Roosters. Nick started out as a nipper, standing on a box to help his dad carve up joints. Instead of a Playstation for his birthday, he got a baby cow, which he reared himself and sold at auction. When there's that much passion put into the ingredients you taste the difference.

### Ingredients

- 600g sweet potato, 2cm thick wedges
- 250g cherry tomatoes, halved lengthways
- ½ bulb garlic (about 6 cloves)
- olive oil
- ¾ tsp fresh rosemary leaves, finely chopped
- ½ tsp chilli flakes
- ½ tsp dried oregano
- 300g rump steak
- 60g mixed baby leaf salad
- salt and black pepper

### Here's how...

**1** Preheat your oven to 220°C/Gas Mark 7. Wash and chop your **sweet potato** in half lengthways (no need to peel). Rest the flat part on a board and slice into each half lengthways and at an angle to make 2cm thick wedges. Chop the **cherry tomatoes** in half lengthways.

**2** Toss the wedges and **garlic** (leave the cloves whole and skin on) in 1 tbsp **olive oil**, ½ tsp **salt** and a grind of **black pepper**. Lay them flat on a baking tray with the **rosemary leaves** scattered over and roast on the top shelf for around 25–30 mins, or until a little crispy at the edges.

**3** Mix 2 tbsp **olive oil** with the **chilli flakes**, **dried oregano**, ¼ tsp **salt** and a few grinds of **black pepper**. Pour this **dressing** into a bowl and add your halved **cherry tomatoes**.

**4** Pat your **steak** dry with some kitchen towel, then heat a non-stick pan on your hob until it's very hot. Season the **steak** on each side with ¼ tsp **salt** and a good grind of **black pepper**. Add 1 tbsp **olive oil** to the pan and when it's almost smoking, fry the **steak**. The cooking time depends on the thickness of your **steak** and how cooked you like it. We like ours medium, which would be 2–3 mins on each side, without touching it in between, for a 2cm thick **steak**.

**5** Once cooked, remove your **steak** from the pan and let it rest on a plate for at least 3 mins, covered with foil if you have some. Your **sweet potato** should be done (crispy on the outside and soft in the middle) by now, so take it out of your oven. Squeeze the **garlic** from its skin (be careful, it's hot) and mix it in with your **sweet potato** to get the **potato** covered in the softened **garlic**. If you're not a huge **garlic** fan, you can use less.

**6** Slice your rested **steak** into 1cm thick slices, making sure you cut against the grain of your **steak**.

**7** On each plate, mix the **salad leaves** with your **cherry tomatoes** and some of the dressing. Top with your **steak slices** and drizzle over the rest of your **dressing**. Serve with your **roasted sweet potato** on the side.

# MID-WEEK MAKE-AWAY SWEET & SOUR PORK
## – WITH BULGUR WHEAT –

**READY IN 30 MINS**        **SERVES** (2)

We love a good 'make-away'…the homemade, healthier, tastier version of a take-away. For this recipe I recommend using pork steaks or chops. Basically a cut that has a little more fat so you can add a boost of flavour. We're also using a Far Eastern favourite called ketjap manis. If 'ketjap' sounds familiar it's because it's like a Indonesian version of our ketchup. Who knew?!

### Ingredients

- 1 vegetable stock pot
- 150g cracked bulgur wheat
- 1 garlic clove, finely chopped
- 1 red pepper, 2cm dice
- 1 yellow pepper, 2cm dice
- 3 spring onions, ½cm discs
- 250g pork steak/chop, bite-sized pieces
- 1 tbsp cornflour
- flavourless oil
- 1 tbsp rice vinegar
- 3 tbsp ketjap manis
- salt and black pepper

### Here's how...

**1** Put a saucepan of 300ml water over a high heat with the **stock pot** and stir to dissolve the **stock pot**. Add the **bulgur wheat** and bring to the boil. When boiling, cover with a lid, take off the heat and leave to rest for 15 mins.

**2** Meanwhile, prep the **garlic**, **peppers** and **spring onions**.

**3** Cut the **pork** into bite-sized pieces. Remember to wash your hands afterwards. Sprinkle the **cornflour** into a mixing bowl and add ½ tsp **salt** and a good grind of **black pepper**. Add the **pork** and toss to coat thoroughly.

**4** Put 1½ tbsp **oil** in a frying pan over a high heat. Line a plate with some paper towel. When the pan is hot, add half the **pork**. Stir-fry until browned, 4 mins. Transfer to a plate lined with paper towel to absorb any excess oil. Add a little more **oil** to the pan and fry the remaining **pork** in the same way. Stir-frying the **pork** in batches means it gets crispy and doesn't stew.

**5** Mix the **rice vinegar** with the **ketjap manis**. Wipe out the frying pan you used for the **pork** with a paper towel, add 1 tbsp **oil** and put it over a medium heat. Stir-fry the **peppers** for 4 mins. Add the **garlic** and half the **spring onions**. Cook for another minute. Stir in the **ketjap manis** mixture and bring to a simmer.

**6** Return the **pork** to the pan and stir thoroughly. Continue cooking for 2–3 mins until the pork is cooked through and no longer pink in the middle. Taste and season with more **salt** and **black pepper** if needed. Serve the **sweet and sour pork** on top of the **bulgur wheat** and sprinkle over the rest of the **spring onions**.

# SPEEDY SICILIAN STEW
## – WITH HERBED PORK & GARLIC CIABATTA –

⏱ **READY IN 40 MINS**　　　　　　**SERVES** ②

Cooking from scratch doesn't need to be hard work. There are a few little shortcuts (not cheats) that can add a hit of depth to your dish without keeping you waiting. Sausage meat is one of those shortcuts. Pre-seasoned and with a delicious, moist texture, it's fantastic for meatballs, on top of pizzas or for this super-quick Sicilian stew. Your guests will think it's been slow-cooking all day…and who are we to say otherwise?

*Ingredients*

- ½ **stick celery**, ½cm dice
- 1 **red pepper**, 2cm dice
- 1 **green pepper**, 2cm dice
- 2 **garlic cloves**, one finely chopped, one halved
- 1 **aubergine**, 2cm dice
- **olive oil**
- 4 regular size **pork sausages** (ideally flavoured with oregano and/or chilli flakes)
- 2 tbsp pitted **green olives**, finely chopped
- 1 tin **chopped tomatoes**
- 1 tbsp **white wine vinegar**
- 3 tbsp fresh **flat leaf parsley**, finely chopped
- 1 small **ciabatta**
- **salt and black pepper**

*Here's how…*

**1** Preheat your oven to 220°C/Gas Mark 7. Prep the **celery** and **peppers**. Finely chop one of the **garlic cloves**. Trim the top and bottom off the **aubergine** and discard. Cut the **aubergine** in half lengthways, then slice each half lengthways into 2cm thick slices. Now line up the slices and chop widthways into 2cm dice.

**2** In a bowl, coat your **aubergine** and **peppers** in 1 tbsp **olive oil**. Spread evenly on a baking tray and roast on the top shelf of your oven for 20 mins, or until a little crispy around the edges.

**3** Heat 1½ tbsp **olive oil** in a large non-stick frying pan over a medium heat. Once hot, add your **celery** and **garlic** with ¼ tsp **salt** and a few grinds of **black pepper**. Whilst this cooks, slice open the **sausages**, discard the skin and add the **meat** to the pan. Break it up and cook for 5 mins. Finely chop the **olives**.

**4** Tip in the **chopped tomatoes** and then refill the tin a quarter with water. Swill the water around and add this to your sauce. Add another ¼ tsp **salt**, the **olives** and the **white wine vinegar**. Leave to simmer and thicken for 10–15 mins.

**5** Once your **veggies** have roasted, remove from your oven and add to the pan and stir. Turn your grill to high.

**6** Cut the **ciabatta** in half and toast on each side under your grill. Once toasted, peel your remaining **garlic clove** and cut it in half. Rub your **garlic** across the cut surface of each **ciabatta** half. Drizzle over a little **olive oil** and a bit of **salt** (less than ¼ tsp). Cut each half in half again.

**7** Once your **stew** has thickened, serve in warm bowls. It can be eaten with cutlery or by using your **ciabatta** as a small edible shovel.

# A SURPRISE SINGAPORE STIR-FRY
## – WITH SHREDDED BEEF & SEASONAL CORN –

🌓 **READY IN 35 MINS**　　　　　　　**SERVES** ②

Winston Churchill once said, 'Fail to prepare, prepare to fail.' We're pretty sure it wasn't cooking related, but the wisdom still rings true. For this recipe you'll have a bit of prep to do upfront, but once the cooking is underway it'll all happen in a flash.

### *Ingredients*

- 1 garlic clove, finely chopped
- ½ red chilli, finely chopped
- 1 green pepper, ½cm slices
- 1 carrot, ½cm wide sticks
- 4 tbsp fresh coriander, roughly chopped
- 1 pak choi, 1cm slices
- 1 corn on the cob
- 220g rump steak, sliced into very thin ribbons
- 2 tbsp ketjap manis
- 1 tbsp rice vinegar
- 1 lime
- 1 nest medium egg noodles
- 2 tbsp plain flour
- 2 tbsp sesame oil
- 2 tsp sesame seeds
- salt and black pepper

### *Here's how...*

**1** Prep the **garlic, chilli, green pepper, carrot** and **coriander**. Chop the base (about 1cm off the end) from the **pak choi** and discard before chopping the remainder widthways into 1cm pieces.

**2** Place the **corn** vertically on your chopping board (i.e. with the base on the board) and rest your hand on top. Run your knife downwards to chop the **corn** from the **cob**. Mind it doesn't ping all over the place.

**3** Slice your **steak** into very thin ribbons (only a few mm thick if poss). Mix the **ketjap manis** and **rice vinegar** in a cup. Zest half of the **lime** and keep the **zest** to the side, then cut the **lime** in half and squeeze half its **juice** into the cup as well. Mix together well.

**4** Put a medium pan of water with ½ tsp **salt** over a high heat. Once it comes to a boil, cook the **noodles** according to the packet instructions before draining them and putting back in the pan with some cold water (this will stop them from overcooking).

**5** Toss the **steak** in a bowl with the **plain flour**, ½ tsp **salt** and a few grinds of **black pepper**. Put a frying pan over a medium–high heat and add 1 tbsp **sesame oil**. Once it's really hot, add the **steak**. Stir-fry it until it's just browned off on the outside (this should take a couple of mins) then put on a plate for later.

**6** Heat the other 1 tbsp **sesame oil** in a non-stick frying pan over a medium–high heat and, once it's nice and hot, add in the **corn, chilli** and **garlic**. Cook for 1 min (the **corn** may start to pop) then add the **carrot** and **peppers**. Cook for 3 mins before adding the **pak choi** for a couple of mins.

**7** Pour in the **ketjap manis** mixture together with the **steak** and give everything a gentle stir before tossing in the drained **noodles** and **coriander**. Slice the remaining half of the **lime** and serve your stir-fry with a sprinkle of **sesame seeds** and the **lime slices**.

## Hello
## STEAK

Put your steak in the freezer
for 30 mins before slicing to
make it easier to slice thinly.

# ORECCHIETTE

## – WITH HERBED PORK, TENDERSTEM, CHILLI & PESTO –

**READY IN 25 MINS**                **SERVES** ②

Though it hasn't yet been medically defined, 'hangriness' is a real affliction (suffered not only by the person with 'hanger', but also all those in their near vicinity). You will recognise the symptoms by displays of heightened emotion, over-reaction and irrationality. This recipe was created with those people in mind. Quick and soothing!

### Ingredients

- 150g tenderstem broccoli, chopped into 3 pieces
- 200g orecchiette pasta
- 200g best-quality pork sausages (about 4)
- olive oil
- ¼ tsp chilli flakes
- 2 tbsp ready-made green pesto
- 1½ tbsp pine nuts
- salt and black pepper

### Here's how...

**1** Put a large pan of water with 1 tbsp **salt** over a high heat and bring to the boil.

**2** Chop each piece of **tenderstem broccoli** into three pieces.

**3** Cook the **tenderstem broccoli** in the boiling water for 1 min. Remove from the water but keep the water for the **orecchiette**.

**4** Cook the **orecchiette pasta** in the water for 10 mins. Reserve 4 tbsp of the **pasta** water (as we'll use this later for the sauce) then drain.

**5** Cut open the **sausages**, take the **meat** out and discard the skins. Heat 2 tsp **olive oil** in a non-stick pan over a medium–high heat. Once hot, add the **sausage meat** breaking it up as you go. Cook for around 5 mins until nicely browned off.

**6** Add the **tenderstem broccoli** and **chilli flakes** (add the **chilli flakes** slowly and taste as you go along) and cook for 2 mins. Season with ¼ tsp **salt** and a few grinds of **black pepper**.

**7** Add the 4 tbsp of reserved **pasta water** then add the **pasta**. Add 2 tbsp **pesto** and stir. Test for seasoning and add a little more **salt** and **black pepper** if you need. Serve with a sprinkle of **pine nuts**.

# MINTED LAMB & FETA BURGERS
## – WITH A CRUNCHY SUMMER SALAD –

🕐 **READY IN 45 MINS**　　　　　　　**SERVES** ②

For Da Vinci, it was Mona Lisa. For Banksy, Kate Moss. Down the centuries great artists have been moved to great feats of creativity by a beautiful muse. For us, that mythical muse is the burger. A thing of such delicious, dribble-down-your-chin simplicity, it can be reinvented time and time again to create the most divine dinnertime results. For this little incarnation, we've taken lamb mince and thrown in a Greek twist and a kick of minty freshness.

## *Ingredients*

- **500g potatoes**, 2cm thick wedges
- **olive oil**
- **½ onion**, thin half moons
- **1 baby gem lettuce**, very thinly chopped widthways
- **125g radishes**, ½cm discs
- **2 spring onions**, ½cm discs
- **2 tbsp fresh mint**, finely chopped
- **¼ tsp sugar**
- **250g lamb mince**
- **2 tbsp panko breadcrumbs**
- **100g feta**, crumbled
- **2 brioche burger buns**, halved
- **salt and black pepper**

## *Here's how...*

**1** Preheat your oven to 220°C/Gas Mark 7. Wash and chop your **potatoes** in half lengthways (no need to peel). Rest the flat part on a board and slice into each half lengthways and at an angle to make 2cm thick wedges. Toss the wedges in 1 tbsp **olive oil**, ½ tsp **salt** and a grind of **black pepper**. Lay them flat on a baking tray and roast on the top shelf for around 25 mins, or until a little crispy at the edges. Prep the **onion, lettuce, radishes, spring onions** and **mint**.

**2** Heat 1½ tbsp **olive oil** in a small frying pan over a low heat. Add the **onion** with ¼ tsp **salt** and the **sugar**. Put a lid on and gently stew for at least 20 mins. The **onion** is ready when it is soft and this will be your **onion relish**.

**3** Next, add the **lamb mince** to a bowl with the **panko breadcrumbs**, half the **mint**, three-quarters of the **spring onions**, ¼ tsp **salt** and a few grinds of **black pepper**. Crumble in half the **feta**.

**4** Mix everything thoroughly with your hands to incorporate all the ingredients. Form the mixture into two equal-sized burger patties. They should be ever so slightly wider than your **buns**, as they'll shrink back when you cook them.

**5** Heat 1 tbsp **olive oil** in a non-stick frying pan over a medium heat. Once hot, add the **burgers** and cook for 6–8 mins on each side. Only turn the **burgers** once and do it gently to avoid breaking them. The **burgers** are cooked when they are no longer pink in the middle. If there is excess liquid coming from the **burger**, simply remove this from the pan with a spoon and discard. You may like to do this a few times.

**6** Once the **potato wedges** are cooked, **turn the oven down to 150°C/ Gas Mark 2**. In a bowl mix the remaining **spring onions** with the **radishes**, **lettuce** and remaining **feta**. Drizzle over 2 tsp **olive oil**, a bit of **salt** (less than ¼ tsp) and some **black pepper**. Add the remaining **mint** and lightly mix with your fingertips.

**7** Split each **brioche bun** in half and put in the oven for 2 mins. Serve the **burgers** in the **buns** with a spoonful of the **onion relish** and the crunchy **salad** and **wedges** on the side.

# HONEY MUSTARD SAUSAGES
## – WITH SWEET POTATO MASH & RED ONION GRAVY –

**READY IN 35 MINS**          **SERVES** (2)

I hesitate to call this one a recipe as it's so ludicrously easy. I think instead we'll call it dinnertime inspiration. Much like in Italian cooking, the secret here is that although there are only a handful of ingredients, the quality of those ingredients is key. Treat yourself to some really lovely sausages to crown that smashing mash and this one will seem more than the sum of its parts.

*Ingredients*

- 4 honey mustard sausages (or just really good pork sausages)
- olive oil
- 600g sweet potato, peeled and cut into 3cm dice
- 300g potatoes, peeled and cut into 3cm dice
- 1 red onion, thin half moons
- 5 tsp butter
- ½ beef stock cube
- 150g tenderstem broccoli
- salt and black pepper

*Here's how...*

**1** Preheat your oven to 200°C/Gas Mark 6. Put a large pan of water over a high heat and bring to the boil.

**2** Put the **sausages** on a lightly oiled baking tray. Roast on the top shelf for 25 mins. Turn halfway through cooking. The **sausages** are cooked when no longer pink in the middle.

**3** Prep the **potatoes** and add to your boiling water. Cook until soft enough to eat, 10–15 mins. **Tip: The potatoes are ready when you can easily slip a knife through them.** Prep the **red onion**. Heat 1½ tbsp **olive oil** in a frying pan over a medium–low heat. Cook the **onion** until soft, stirring frequently for 10 mins.

**4** Once the **sweet** and **potatoes** are cooked, drain them and retain the water in another pan to use for your **gravy**. Return the **potatoes** to the pan, add 2 tsp **butter** with ½ tsp **salt** and, with the back of a fork or a potato masher, mash it for all you're worth.

**5** Put another pan of water over a high heat and bring to the boil. Add 150ml of your reserved **potato water** into your **onions** together with the ½ **beef stock cube** and the remaining **butter**. **Tip: If you have any red wine, add a splash at this point for extra flavour.** Bring up to the boil and simmer until your **gravy** has reduced and thickened. Simply add a splash more water if it goes too thick, and if you're feeling decadent, add extra **butter** too.

**6** Cook the **tenderstem broccoli** in the pan of boiling water until tender, 3–4 mins. Drain in a colander when done.

**7** Serve your **sausages** and **mash** with your **tenderstem broccoli** and a spoonful of **onion gravy**.

# BODY-BOOSTING HOISIN PORK

## – WITH BROWN RICE, YELLOW PEPPER & SUGARSNAP PEAS –

**READY IN 35 MINS**          **SERVES** ②

Traditionally, January has always been a big month at HelloFresh. We call it our Fresh Start month, with so many people ordering recipe boxes to kickstart their year. This recipe has always been a January favourite, though you definitely don't need to wait for a new year for a Fresh Start.

### Ingredients

- 150g brown basmati rice
- ½ red onion, thin half moons
- 2 garlic cloves, finely chopped
- ½ red chilli, finely chopped
- 3 tbsp fresh coriander, roughly chopped
- ½ stick celery, ½cm pieces
- 1 tbsp fresh ginger, peeled and chopped
- 1 yellow pepper, 2cm dice
- 200g pork loin, cut into 2cm pieces
- 1 tbsp cornflour
- flavourless oil
- 120g sugarsnap peas
- 2 limes, one halved and one in wedges
- 3 tbsp hoisin sauce
- salt and black pepper

### Here's how...

**1** Bring a large pan of water to a rapid boil with ½ tsp **salt**. Wash the **rice** under running water for 30 seconds. Add your **rice** to the pan and cook for 25 mins, topping up the water when it begins to evaporate. Once the **rice** is cooked, drain and leave to one side.

**2** Prep the **red onion, garlic, red chilli, coriander, celery, ginger** and **yellow pepper**.

**3** Cut the **pork** into 2cm pieces, then dab it dry with paper towel. Toss your **pork** in the **cornflour** together with ¼ tsp **salt** and a few grinds of **black pepper**.

**4** Heat 1½ tbsp **oil** in a non-stick frying pan over a high heat. Once really hot, carefully add your **pork** (it might sputter a bit). Stir-fry your **pork** for 3 mins, until cooked through and no longer pink in the middle. Remove your **pork** from the pan and cover in foil to keep warm.

**5** Heat 1 tbsp **oil** to the now empty pan and add your **onion, garlic, chilli** and **ginger**. After 1 min, add your **pepper** and cook for 2 mins more. Add the **sugarsnap peas** and your **celery** and cook for 1 min. Add 3 tbsp water, cover the pan and cook for another 2 mins.

**6** Cut one of your **limes** in half and squeeze its **juice** into the **hoisin sauce**. Cut the other **lime** into wedges to serve with the **stir-fry**. Take the lid off your **veggies** and add your **hoisin sauce** together with your **pork**. Toss everything together for 1 min. Plate your **stir-fry** on top of your **brown rice**, sprinkle with **coriander** and serve with **lime wedges** on the side.

# MIXED BEAN & PORK CHILLI

## – WITH BROWN RICE & CITRUS SOURED CREAM –

**READY IN 30 MINS**    **SERVES** (2)

Come along to the HelloFresh Farm one lunchtime and you'll see a huge family table with people munching happily away on the HelloFresh recipe they cooked the night before. The really clever ones have a system: they pair up and one person cooks for both of them one day, then they swap. It's created some heartwarming couplings. This recipe is a favourite since it only gets more flavourful for spending a night marinating in the fridge.

*Ingredients*

- 150g brown rice
- ½ red onion, thin half moons
- ½ tin mixed beans, drained and rinsed
- ½ lime, zest and juice
- 75g soured cream
- olive oil
- 250g best-quality pork sausages
- 1½ tsp ground cumin
- 1 tbsp tomato purée
- ½ tbsp chipotle paste (or powder)
- 1 tin chopped tomatoes
- 1 vegetable stock pot
- 3 tbsp fresh coriander, roughly chopped
- salt and black pepper

*Here's how...*

**1** Put a large saucepan of water over a high heat with ½ tsp **salt** and bring to the boil. Rinse the **rice** in a sieve under running water for 30 seconds, then add it to your pan of rapidly boiling water. Cook until the **rice** is soft, 25–30 mins (adding water if it evaporates). Drain and return to the pan. over with a lid and leave off the heat until the **chilli** is cooked.

**2** Prep the **red onion**. Drain and rinse the **mixed beans** in a colander. Zest and juice the **lime**. **Tip: When zesting, don't go down to the white part underneath the skin as this tastes bitter.** Mix half of the **zest** and half of the **juice** into the **soured cream**.

**3** Heat 1 tbsp **olive oil** in a frying pan over a medium–high heat. Cut open the **sausages** at the end and squeeze out the **meat** into the frying pan (discard the skins). Cook the **sausage meat** until brown, 5–7 mins. Use a wooden spoon to break up the **sausage meat** as it cooks.

**4** Add the **onion** to the pan, along with ¼ tsp **salt** and a few grinds of **black pepper**. Stir, then cook until the **onion** has softened, about 5 mins. Add the **cumin**. Cook until fragrant, 1 min. Then add the **tomato purée** and **chipotle paste** (careful – it's hot).

**5** Add the **mixed beans**, the **tomatoes** and the **vegetable stock pot**. Stir to dissolve the **stock pot** and then bring to the boil. Turn down the heat and gently bubble until the **chilli** has thickened and reduced by half, 7–10 mins. While you wait, chop the **coriander leaves**, discarding the stalks.

**6** Stir the remaining **lime zest** through the **rice**. Then serve your **chilli** with the **rice**, the **zesty soured cream**, a sprinkling of chopped **coriander** and the extra **lime juice** if you like.

## Hello
## CHILLI

People customise their chilli with
all sorts of 'secret' ingredients: dark
chocolate, even Marmite or Bovril.
We like to throw in chipotle for
a smokey hit. What's your 'secret'?

# PEANUTTY PORK BURGERS

## – WITH AN UNCTUOUS SATAY SAUCE –

Nothing is left to chance in the HelloFresh Kitchen. Mimi and André toil day by day to tinker and tweak the recipes to perfection. From there everyone has a chance to come down to the kitchen and give them a test cook under the watchful eye of Lizzie. It's a tough life (!), but if we need to taste test a burger like this ten times before we let it go in a box, then that's what we're willing to do. Ahem.

**READY IN 40 MINS**

**SERVES** ②

## Ingredients

- 500g **sweet potato,** 2cm wedges
- **olive oil**
- 2 tsp mild smoked **paprika**
- 4 tbsp fresh **coriander,** finely chopped
- 40g salted **peanuts,** roughly chopped
- 300g **pork mince**
- 1 **lime,** zest and juice
- 1½ tbsp **soy sauce**
- 40g crunchy **peanut butter**
- 1 baby gem **lettuce,** 1cm widthways strips
- 1 **carrot,** grated
- 2 brioche **burger buns,** halved
- **salt** and **black pepper**

## Here's how...

**1** Preheat the oven to 220°C/425°F/Gas Mark 7. Wash and chop your **sweet potatoes** in half lengthways (no need to peel). Rest the flat part on a board and slice into each half lengthways and at an angle to make 2cm thick wedges. Toss the wedges in 1 tbsp of **olive oil,** ½ tsp of **salt,** a grind of **black pepper** and half the **paprika.** Lay them flat on a baking tray and roast on the top shelf for around 25 mins, or until a little crispy at the edges

**2** Prep the **coriander** and **peanuts.** Put the **pork mince** in a bowl and add three-quarters of your **coriander** along with ¼ tsp of **lime** zest, the **peanuts,** the other half of your **paprika,** half the **soy sauce** and a good grind of **black pepper.**

**3** Combine everything together with your hands. Form the mixture into two equal-sized burger patties. They should be ever so slightly wider than your **buns,** as they'll shrink back when you cook them.

**4** Add 1½ tbsp **olive oil** to a frying pan over a medium heat and cook your **burgers,** 5 mins on each side. Then place them on a baking tray in the oven for 4 mins. For the last 2 mins of cooking, halve the **burger buns** and put them in the oven too.

**5** Mix together the **peanut butter,** half the **lime** juice, 2 tbsp water, the remaining **soy sauce** and **coriander** in a bowl with a fork. Add more **lime** zest and juice to your liking.

**6** Remove and discard the tough rooty bit of the **lettuce** and chop into roughly 1cm strips. Peel and grate the **carrot,** then mix it with your **lettuce** in a bowl. Pour over 1 tbsp of **olive oil** and the remaining **lime** juice. Season with a bit of **salt** (less than ¼ tsp) and a few grinds of **black pepper.**

**7** When everything is ready, serve your **burgers** on the satay sauce in the **buns,** topped with the **lettuce** and **carrot,** and with the **sweet potato wedges** on the side.

# RACHEL'S ITALIAN PORK & TOMATO RISOTTO

🕐 **READY IN 40 MINS**　　　　　　　　　**SERVES** ②

*Ingredients*

- 1 chicken stock pot
- 200g tomato passata
- 1 onion, ½cm dice
- 1 garlic clove, finely chopped
- 3 tbsp fresh flat leaf parsley, roughly chopped
- 250g pork sausages (the best you can find)
- 80g Parmesan, grated
- olive oil
- 2–3 tbsp butter
- 175g arborio rice
- 1 tsp fennel seeds
- 4 tbsp white wine or 2 tbsp white wine vinegar (optional)
- salt and black pepper

Being in my little kitchen for the first couple of years of HelloFresh was a pretty solitary pursuit, so I advertised for a sous chef at Le Cordon Bleu. Only one person replied, but she was perfect. Every Monday she'd take a day off work (as a chartered accountant) to help me in the kitchen. Thank you Rachel, you can't imagine how much your hard work and friendship meant to me. This recipe is one of her many winners.

## *Here's how...*

**1** Put a pan of 800ml water over a medium heat and bring to a simmer. Once simmering, add the **chicken stock pot** and **tomato passata** and stir thoroughly. Turn the heat down and keep on the lowest heat during the whole cooking process.

**2** Prep the **onion** and **garlic**. Roughly chop the **parsley** (stalks and all). Cut open the **sausages**, take the **meat** out and discard the skins. Break the **sausage meat** into small bite-sized pieces. Grate the **Parmesan**.

**3** Heat 1 tbsp **olive oil** in a large saucepan over a low heat with 1 tbsp **butter**. Add the **onion** with ¼ tsp **salt** and cook for 5 mins, then add the **garlic** and cook for 1 min. Add the **sausage meat** and cook for 3 mins. Add the **arborio rice** and **fennel seeds** (add less **fennel** if you don't love the aniseedy flavour). Stir together to make sure the **rice** is coated in **oil** and cook for 2 mins.

**4** If you have some **white wine**, add 4 tbsp now. Let the alcohol in the **wine** bubble off for a few minutes to mellow the flavour. If you don't have any wine don't worry, you can use 2 tbsp **white wine vinegar** or just move right on to step 5. The **risotto** will still taste delicious.

**5** Add a ladleful of the **stock and passata mix** to the **rice** and stir in long, continuous motions. Once the liquid is almost fully absorbed, add another ladleful and continue stirring. Keep adding the **stock and passata mix**, stirring all the time until the **rice** is cooked, about 25 mins. **Tip: We like our risotto to have a slight firmness in the middle of the rice. If you want to cook it more but don't have any stock left, you can add a few more tbsp of water.**

**6** Once your **risotto** is ready, stir in the **Parmesan** and remaining **butter** (which will loosen it up and give it a beautiful glossy look). The ideal **risotto** should flow like lava. Serve in warm bowls with a sprinkling of **parsley** and extra **Parmesan** (if you like) and eat immediately.

# COLD-BUSTING MEXICAN SOUP
## – WITH SPICY BEEF & BEANS –

**READY IN 45 MINS**                    **SERVES** (2)

As you can probably guess, this one is a wintertime favourite. Y'see the first HelloFresh Farm (AKA our HQ) was a fairly, ummm, intimate place. We were growing at a rate of knots, so every day a new desk got added to an increasingly pokey room. It was definitely cosy, but the downside was that when one person got a cold we all ended up sharing it. I created this Mexican penicillin so that we could hold on to that office just a little bit longer.

*You can freeze the rest in twos for later, they keep really well.

### Ingredients

- 1 onion, ½cm dice
- 1 garlic clove, finely chopped
- 1 green pepper, 1cm dice
- 2 tomatoes, 1cm dice
- 1 tin mixed beans, drained and rinsed
- 300g potatoes, ½cm dice
- 3 tbsp fresh coriander, roughly chopped
- olive oil
- 250g beef mince
- 1 tbsp Mexican/fajita spice
- 1½ tsp mild paprika
- 200ml tomato passata
- 1 beef stock pot
- 1 wholemeal tortilla*
- 5 tbsp soured cream
- salt and black pepper

### Here's how...

**1** Preheat your oven to 200°/Gas Mark 6. Prep the **onion, garlic, green pepper** and **tomatoes**. Drain and thoroughly rinse the **mixed beans**. Peel and chop the **potatoes** into ½cm dice (they need to be small to ensure they cook through). Separate the **coriander** leaves from their stalks. Finely chop both the stalks and the leaves and keep separate.

**2** Heat 1½ tbsp **olive oil** in a large saucepan over a medium heat. Once hot, add the **onion**. Cook gently for 4 mins. Then add the **mince** and cook for 2 mins. Then add the **coriander stalks, garlic, Mexican spice** (less if you don't want it very spicy) and **mild paprika** with ½ tsp **salt** and a good grind of **black pepper**. Cook until the **mince** is just browned (about 3 mins whilst stirring).

**3** Once the **mince** has browned, add the **pepper, tomatoes** and **potatoes**. Cook until softened, 4 mins. Add the **mixed beans** along with the **tomato passata**. Simmer gently for 2 mins.

**4** Add the **beef stock pot** together with 500ml water. Bring to a very gentle boil, then lower the heat. Simmer until the **potatoes** are cooked through, 15–20 mins. If the **stock** is reducing too much, add a splash more water.

**5** When the **soup** is 10 mins from done, rub a very light coating of **oil** onto both sides of the **tortilla**. Slice into long (1cm wide) strips. Season with ¼ tsp **salt**, some **black pepper** and place on a baking tray on the top shelf of your oven. Cook for 4–5 mins, until crispy. Watch them like a hawk as they burn easily.

**6** Just before serving, stir through half the **coriander leaves**. Taste and add more **salt** and **black pepper** if you need. Serve the **soup** in bowls, topped with the **soured cream**, a little more **coriander** and some of your **crispy tortilla chips**. Get slurping!

# SPEEDY RIGATONI

## – WITH CHERRY TOMATOES & MOZZARELLA –

**READY IN 30 MINS**          **SERVES** ②

It's an incredible thing to see passionate chefs plying their trade in a busy kitchen. The flow of a busy lunchtime service is like a choreographed dance, as they create beauty on auto-pilot. I remember seeing that dance in my favourite restaurant in the world 'Da Gino' in Rome. One of their tricks was to take a ladleful of pasta water and use it as the base to make a silky pasta sauce. Simplicity can be so magical!

### Ingredients

- 1 red pepper, 1cm strips
- 1 yellow pepper, 1cm strips
- 250g cherry tomatoes, halved lengthways
- olive oil
- 1 onion, ½cm dice
- 2 garlic cloves, finely chopped
- 10 medium size fresh basil leaves, roughly chopped
- 200g dry rigatoni pasta (or penne)
- 60g chorizo, 1cm dice
- 2 tbsp pitted black olives, sliced lengthways
- 1 ball mozzarella cheese, torn into bite-sized pieces
- salt and black pepper

### Here's how...

**1** Preheat your oven to 200°C/Gas Mark 6. Put a large saucepan of water with 1 tbsp **salt** over a high heat and bring to the boil for the **pasta**.

**2** Prep the **peppers** and cut the **cherry tomatoes** in half lengthways. Lay the **tomatoes** and **peppers** on a baking tray, drizzle with 1 tbsp **olive oil**, season with ¼ tsp **salt** and toss together. Roast on the top shelf of your oven until starting to brown at the edges, 15–20 mins.

**3** Prep the **onion**, **garlic** and **basil**.

**4** Add the **rigatoni** to your pan of boiling water. Cook until 'al dente' (cooked through but with a tiny bit of firmness left in the middle), about 11 mins (or according to the packet instructions).

**5** Cut the **chorizo** into 1cm dice. Put 1 tbsp **olive oil** in a frying pan over a medium heat. Once hot, add the **onion** and **chorizo**. Cook until the **onion** is soft, 5 mins. Add the **garlic** and a few good grinds of **black pepper**. Cook for 1 min more.

**6** Cut the **olives** in half lengthways (or roughly chop if you want to save a bit of time) and add to the pan along with 3 tbsp of the **pasta water**.

**7** Once the **pasta** is cooked, drain in a colander and combine with the contents of the frying pan. Add the roasted **tomatoes** and **peppers**. Tear in half the **mozzarella cheese** and add most, but not all, of the chopped **basil**. Serve in bowls with the remaining **mozzarella** torn over the top. Sprinkle with the rest of the **basil** and drizzle over a little **olive oil**. Buon appetito.

# BEEF ENCHILADAS
## – WITH HOMEMADE RANCHERO BEANS –

🕐 **READY IN 40 MINS**　　　　　　　　**SERVES** ②

Rumour has it that a recipe for enchiladas appeared in Mexico's first ever cookbook, which was published way back in 1831. We decided to give it a new spin by mashing the kidney beans to give the sauce a thick, creamy consistency. If you'd like to mix up the presentation, you can also use the soft tortillas to line the inside of small ovenproof bowls and then put them in a hot oven for a few minutes. Take them out and you'll have edible tortilla bowls.

### *Ingredients*

- olive oil
- 250g beef mince
- 1 onion, half moons
- ½ tin kidney beans, drained and rinsed
- 1 tbsp Mexican/fajita spice
- 200ml tomato passata
- 1 baby gem lettuce, roughly chopped
- 2 vine tomatoes, 1cm dice
- 4 wholemeal soft tortillas
- 4 tbsp Cheddar, grated
- 150ml soured cream
- 1 lime, half zested and half cut into wedges
- salt and black pepper

### *Here's how...*

**1** Preheat your oven to 220°C/Gas Mark 7. Put 1½ tbsp **olive oil** in a frying pan over a medium–high heat. Once hot, add the **beef mince** with ½ tsp **salt**. Cook until well browned, 5–6 mins.

**2** Meanwhile, prep the **onion** and add to the pan with the browned **beef**. Cook until soft, 6 mins. Drain and thoroughly rinse the **kidney beans** in a colander. Put them in a mixing bowl and mash with a potato masher or the back of a fork. Once the **onion** is soft, add the **fajita seasoning** (add a bit less if you don't want it very spicy). Cook for 1 min more.

**3** Add the **tomato passata** and ¼ tsp **salt**. Refill the **passata** container with just over 2 tbsp water, swirl it around and add this too. Add the **beans** to your pan and let the mixture simmer gently over a medium–low heat until it has reduced by half and is lovely and thick. Meanwhile, roughly chop the **baby gem lettuce** and dice the **vine tomatoes**.

**4** Once the mixture is thick, take it off the heat. Spoon equal amounts down one side of each **tortilla**. Roll the **tortillas** up into cylinders and place them in an ovenproof dish. Pack them snugly, side by side, with the folded edge downwards so they don't unroll. Grate over the **Cheddar**. Place on the top shelf of your oven and bake until the **Cheddar** melts.

**5** Whilst the enchiladas are in your oven, put the **soured cream** in a small bowl. Grate in 1 tsp of the **lime zest** and add a few good grinds of **black pepper**. Mix well. Add more if you like things citrussy.

**6** In another mixing bowl, toss the **baby gem lettuce** and **tomatoes** with 1 tsp **lime juice** and 1 tbsp **olive oil**. Season with a bit of **salt** (less than ¼ tsp) and a few good grinds of **black pepper**. Serve the **enchiladas** with a dollop of **zesty soured cream** and the **salad** and **lime wedges** on the side. Devour immediately.

# PORK & APPLE BURGER

## – WITH ROSEMARY CHIPS –

🕐 **READY IN 40 MINS**                  **SERVES** ② 

Bert and Ernie, Batman and Robin, Harry and Sally…
there are certain combinations that are just better
together. The marriage of pork and apple falls firmly
into that category and this burger has always been
one of the most demanded by our lovely home cooks.
Our tip is to take the pork out of your fridge around
45 mins before cooking – bringing it up to room
temperature means the burgers cook more evenly.

*Ingredients*

- 2 tsp fresh rosemary leaves, finely chopped
- 500g potatoes, 2cm wedges
- olive oil
- 1 apple, grated
- 250g pork mince
- 2 tbsp panko breadcrumbs
- 60g Cheddar, grated
- 2 brioche burger buns
- 1 tbsp honey
- ½ lemon
- 60g rocket or baby spinach
- 2 tbsp apple sauce
- salt and black pepper

*Here's how...*

**1** Preheat your oven to 220°C/Gas Mark 7. Pick the **rosemary leaves** from
their stalks and finely chop (discard the stalks). Wash your **potatoes** and
chop in half lengthways (no need to peel). Rest the flat part on the
board and slice into each half lengthways and at an angle to make 2cm thick
wedges. Toss the wedges in 1 tbsp **olive oil**, ½ tsp **salt**, a grind of **black
pepper** and the **rosemary**. Lay them flat in a baking tray and roast on the
top shelf for around 25 mins, or until a little crispy at the edges.

**2** Coarsely grate the **apple** (discard the core). Place the grated **apple** in a
clean tea towel and squeeze out as much juice as you can (you don't want
soggy burgers). Put the **pork** in a mixing bowl and add the **apple** and the
**panko breadcrumbs**. Season with ¾ tsp **salt** and a generous grind of **black
pepper**, then mix well. Form the mixture into two equal-sized burger patties.
They should be ever so slightly wider than your **buns**, as they'll shrink back
when you cook them.

**3** Heat 1 tbsp **olive oil** in a frying pan over a medium heat. Once hot, gently
add the **burgers** and cook until no longer pink in the middle, around 12
mins on each side, turning every 4 mins to prevent burning. Don't turn either
**burger** until it has formed a crust on the underside, or it might stick to the
pan.

**4** Meanwhile, grate the **Cheddar**. Once the **burgers** are cooked, take the
pan off the heat. Divide the **Cheddar** between the **burgers** then pop a lid on
the pan and set aside for the **Cheddar** to melt, about 4 mins.

**5** While the **burgers** are cooking, split each **brioche bun** in half. Place on
another baking tray and pop them on the middle shelf of your oven to warm
through for 2 mins. To make the **dressing**, put the **honey** in a large bowl and
add the **juice** of the ½ **lemon** with the same amount of **olive oil**. Season
with a bit of **salt** (less than ¼ tsp) and **black pepper**.

**6** Spread a little **apple sauce** onto each of your **brioche** halves. Serve your
**burgers** in the **buns** with some **potato wedges**. Very gently toss the **salad**
leaves in the **dressing** and serve some on top of the **burger** with the rest on
the side.

# GREEK 'LASAGNE'

For reasons which aren't entirely clear to us, when Mimi was at school she had the nickname 'Mimi Moussaka'. She wasn't so keen on the name and as a result (understandably) refused to eat moussaka. But Mimi's mum was one step ahead of the game, whipping up her arch nemesis and rebranding it as a Greek lasagne. And that's where the love affair began. This dish is an homage to those times. Answers on a postcard if you can figure out the nickname…

**READY IN 40 MINS**

**SERVES** ②

## Ingredients

1 **onion**, 1cm dice

1 **carrot**, 1cm dice

2 **garlic cloves**, one finely chopped, one halved

1 **aubergine**, 1cm discs

**olive oil**

250g **lamb mince**

1 **cinnamon stick**

1 **tin chopped tomatoes**

200ml **tomato passata**

1 small **ciabatta**

100ml **crème fraîche**

2 tbsp **Parmesan**, grated

50g **rocket leaves**

**salt and black pepper**

## Here's how…

**1** Prep the **onion** and **carrot**. Peel and finely chop one of the **garlic** cloves. Trim the top and bottom off the **aubergine** and discard, then slice the **aubergine** into 1cm discs.

**2** Heat 1½ tbsp **olive oil** in a frying pan over a medium heat, add the **onion** and **carrot**. Cook until soft, 6 mins. Add the **garlic** and cook for 1 min. Add the **lamb** and **cinnamon stick**, stir. Cook for 5–6 mins, until the **lamb** has browned (drain the fat now if necessary). Add the **chopped tomatoes** and **passata**. Season with ¼ tsp **salt** and **black pepper**. Simmer for 15–20 mins until thickened.

**3** Meanwhile, preheat your grill to high. Evenly coat the **aubergine** slices in a thin layer of **olive oil**, sprinkle over ¼ tsp **salt** and a few grinds of **black pepper**. Grill, in a lined baking tray, for 8–9 mins on the highest shelf on each side. The **aubergine** should be browned and soft, so grill it for a little longer if necessary. If it is browning too quickly, turn the heat down a little. When ready, remove from your grill and leave to the side (leave your grill on).

**4** While the **lamb** and **aubergine** are cooking, cut the **ciabatta** widthways into 1cm thick slices and leave to the side. When the **lamb** mixture is nice and thick, remove the **cinnamon stick** and pour into an ovenproof dish. Lay the **aubergine** on top and spoon over the **crème fraîche**. Spread the **crème fraîche** with the back of a spoon, then grate over the **Parmesan**. Grill the 'lasagne' for about 5 mins, until the top is bubbling and brown.

**5** While the 'lasagne' is browning, put the **rocket** in a bowl, drizzle over 2 tsp **olive oil**, a bit of **salt** (less than ¼ tsp) and some **black pepper**. Toss together to coat the **rocket**.

**6** Once brown, remove the 'lasagne' from your grill. Pop the **ciabatta** slices under the grill for 2 mins on each side, until toasted. Cut the remaining **garlic clove** in half, remove the **ciabatta** from your grill and rub the **garlic** across each slice. You can also drizzle over a little **olive oil**. Serve the 'lasagne' with the **dressed rocket** and **garlic ciabatta** on the side.

# MIDDLE EASTERN SPICED BEEF RAGOUT

## – WITH COUSCOUS, CORIANDER & FLAKED ALMONDS –

🌗 **READY IN 30 MINS**                    **SERVES** ②

This recipe comes with a little trivia lesson care of our incredible Chef André: 'Ras-el-hanout is a spice mixture used throughout North Africa. Literally translated, the name means "top of the shop". Kind of like our "top drawer", it's the best each spice-seller has to offer and no two merchants have quite the same blend. These days, you don't need to go to North Africa to get some, as you can find a blend easily in larger supermarkets or online. If not, look for another Middle Eastern mix like baharat.'

### Ingredients

- 2 tbsp flaked almonds
- olive oil
- 250g beef mince
- 1 onion, 1cm dice
- 1 garlic clove, finely chopped
- 1 red pepper, ½cm strips
- 3 tbsp fresh coriander, finely chopped
- 1 courgette, 1cm thick discs
- 1 tbsp ras-el-hanout spice
- 1 tin chopped tomatoes
- 1 beef stock pot
- 150g couscous
- salt and black pepper

### Here's how...

**1** Heat a frying pan over a medium–high heat with no oil, add the **flaked almonds** and fry until golden brown, then set aside in a bowl. Heat 1 tbsp **olive oil** in the same frying pan over a high heat. When the **oil** is hot, add the **beef mince**. Break up the **beef** with a wooden spoon and season it with ½ tsp **salt** and a few grinds of **black pepper**. Cook until nicely brown, about 7 mins.

**2** Prep the **onion, garlic, red pepper** and **coriander**. Slice the **courgette** into 1cm thick discs.

**3** Once the **beef** has browned, reduce the heat to medium, add the **onion, pepper** and **ras-el-hanout**. Cook for 5 mins. Add the **garlic** and cook for 1 min more. Pour in the **tomatoes**, then fill the empty tin a quarter full with water and add to the pan with half the **beef stock pot** and ¼ tsp **salt**. Bring to the boil, then reduce the heat to medium–low. Leave the **ragout** to simmer for 20 mins.

**4** Put a saucepan of 300ml water over a high heat, bring to a boil and stir in the remaining half of the **stock pot** with ¼ tsp **salt** and a few grinds of **black pepper**. Add the **couscous**, take off the heat, put a lid on and leave for 10 mins.

**5** Put a separate frying pan over a high heat with no oil. Cook the **courgette** for 4 mins on each side. Once nicely charred, transfer to a plate, season with ¼ tsp **salt** and some **black pepper** and set aside.

**6** Taste the **ragout** and add a little more **salt** and **black pepper** if it needs it, then stir through the **coriander**. Divide the **couscous** between bowls, spoon over the **ragout** and finish with the **charred courgettes** and a sprinkle of **toasted almonds**.

# SPEEDY PENNE ALL'ARRABBIATA

## – WITH FRESH BASIL & PARMESAN –

🕐 **READY IN 25 MINS**                                    **SERVES** ②

Food is described with an infinite number of adjectives but 'angry' isn't usually one of them. Although that's exactly what arrabbiata means in Italian. This dish is so called because of its chilli kick – but we'll leave you to decide how much of a temper you want it to have. Given that this tasty recipe can be ready in the time it takes to boil your pasta, there's really nothing to be angry about. So smile and tuck in.

*Ingredients*

- **2 red peppers,** ½cm strips
- **olive oil**
- **2 garlic cloves,** finely chopped
- **3 tbsp fresh basil,** roughly chopped
- **½ red chilli,** finely chopped
- **75g pancetta** or **smokey bacon,** 1cm strips or cubes
- **1 tbsp balsamic vinegar**
- **200g penne pasta**
- **1 tin chopped tomatoes**
- **3 tbsp Parmesan,** grated
- **salt and black pepper**

*Here's how...*

**1** Preheat your oven to 220°C/Gas Mark 7. Put a large pan of water with 1 tbsp **salt** over a high heat and bring to the boil for the **pasta**. Prep the **peppers** and place on a baking tray. Coat evenly with 1 tbsp **olive oil** and season with ¼ tsp **salt** and a good grind of **black pepper**, then toss together. Cook on the top shelf of your oven for 15 mins.

**2** Prep the **garlic, basil, red chilli** and **pancetta** (if you've bought whole pancetta). If you're making this on the spur of the moment and don't have **pancetta**, you can use a bit of chopped **smokey bacon** instead.

**3** Heat 1 tbsp **olive oil** in a frying pan over a medium heat. Fry the **pancetta** until crispy, around 4 mins. Add the **garlic** and **balsamic vinegar**. Cook together for 1 min, the **vinegar** should evaporate. Add the **tomatoes** and the **chilli** (as much as you dare) and season with ¼ tsp **salt** and a few grinds of **black pepper**. Cook over a medium heat for around 10 mins, until you have a nice thick sauce.

**4** Meanwhile, cook the **penne** in the pan of boiling water for around 11 mins (or according to the packet instructions), until it is 'al dente' (cooked through but with a tiny bit of firmness left in the middle).

**5** Once the **pasta** is cooked, drain it and then stir into the thickened **tomato sauce**. Make sure the **pepper** is nice and soft and add it to the **sauce** too.

**6** Scatter the **basil leaves** over the **pasta**. Grate on the **Parmesan** and dig in. **Tip: Best eaten with a fork, in a reclined position on the sofa.**

# SPICY SAUSAGE CHILLI
## – HOMEMADE TORTILLA CHIPS –

⏱ **READY IN 35 MINS**  **SERVES ②**

We're firm believers in DIY. When we moved into the new HelloFresh Farm (our HQ) we spent weeks coming in beforehand to paint, hammer and saw our new home into existence. Sure, we could have got other people to do the work, but there's a feeling of pride in making it happen yourself. Same goes for this recipe in which you'll be whipping up your own homemade tortilla chips. Served with a side order of accomplishment.

### Ingredients

- 1 leek, 1cm half moons
- 1 garlic clove, finely chopped
- 1 red pepper, 1cm dice
- 3 tbsp fresh chives, finely chopped or snipped
- 4 pork sausages
- olive oil
- 1 tin kidney beans, drained and rinsed
- 1½ tsp smoked paprika
- 1½ tsp ground cumin
- ¼ tsp chilli flakes
- 1 tin chopped tomatoes
- 1 beef stock pot
- 2 soft wholemeal tortillas
- 150g Greek yoghurt
- salt and black pepper

### Here's how...

**1** Prep the **leek**, **garlic** and **pepper**. Chop the chives into ½cm pieces. **Tip: Use scissors to do this if you want.**

**2** Put a large frying pan over a medium–high heat with 1½ tbsp **olive oil**. Add the **leek** and **pepper**. Cook for 6 mins until soft; don't worry if they colour slightly, this will just add to the flavour. Cut the **sausages** open and remove the **meat**, discarding the skin. Drain and rinse the **kidney beans** in a colander.

**3** Once the **pepper** is soft, add the **sausage meat**. Cook until browned, 5 mins. Use a spoon to break it up while it cooks. Add ¼ tsp **salt** and a few grinds of **black pepper**. Add the **garlic**, **smoked paprika**, **cumin** and as many **chilli flakes** as you dare. Cook for 1 min more. Pour in the **tomatoes**. Fill the tin a quarter with water, swirl around and add to the pan as well. Stir in the **beef stock pot** and the **kidney beans**. Cook until thick, 10–12 mins.

**4** While the **chilli** cooks, make the **tortilla chips**. Using some scissors, cut each **tortilla** into eight triangles (we used one **tortilla** per person but if you want to use two per person, go for it).

**5** Place the **tortilla triangles** on a large baking tray in a single layer and rub over a very thin coat of **olive oil**. Sprinkle over a little **salt** and a grind of **black pepper**. Put on the top shelf of your oven for 4–5 mins. Keep an eye on them to make sure they don't burn.

**6** Taste the **chilli** and add more **salt** and **black pepper** if necessary. Serve the **chilli** in bowls with the **yoghurt** on top and a sprinkling of **chives**. Place the **tortilla chips** on the side of the bowl for scooping purposes.

# THAI 'MOO PAD KRAPOW'

⏱ **READY IN 30 MINS**　　　　　　　　　**SERVES** ②

Moo pad what?! I picked this recipe up while I was living in Bangkok. If you ever get the chance to go, then the only places to be are the local food halls. These are all over the city and they're where all the locals go to get their lunch and dinner. Buy yourself a little booklet of tickets at the front desk and then an entire indoor market of local (super-cheap) specialities awaits. If you don't speak Thai then get ready to do lots of pointing and smiling to get what you want…or just repeat after me: Moo Pad Krapow.

*Ingredients*

- 150g white basmati rice
- 1 echalion shallot (the long one), ½cm dice
- 2 garlic cloves, finely chopped
- ¼ red chilli, finely chopped
- 3 spring onions, ½cm discs
- 150g green beans, trimmed and halved
- flavourless oil
- 300g pork mince
- 2 tbsp ketjap manis (sweet soy sauce)
- 2 tbsp Chinese soy sauce
- 3 tbsp Thai basil*, torn
- salt and black pepper

*Here's how…*

**1** Put a pan of 300ml water with ¼ tsp **salt** over a high heat and bring to the boil. When boiling, add the **rice**, lower the heat to medium and put on a lid. Cook for 10 mins, then remove from the pan from the heat and set aside (still covered) for another 10 mins. **Tip: Do not touch the lid until at least 20 mins are up or the rice will not cook properly.**

**2** Prep the **shallot, garlic, red chilli** (as much as you dare) and **spring onions**. Trim the ends from the **green beans**, then cut the **green beans** in half.

**3** Put 1 tbsp **oil** in a frying pan over a high heat. Once hot, add the **green beans** and stir-fry until tender, 2–3 mins. When cooked, transfer to a plate.

**4** Keep the pan over a high heat and add another tbsp **oil**. Add the **pork** and stir-fry until browned and cooked through, 6–8 mins. Break it up with a wooden spoon as it cooks. When the **pork** is cooked, add the **shallot, garlic, spring onions** and as much **chilli** as you fancy. Cook until the **veggies** are softened, another 2–3 mins.

**5** Return the **green beans** to the pan. Add the **ketjap manis** and **soy sauce** and stir everything together. If the **mixture** is a little dry add a splash of water.

**6** Remove the **pork** from the heat and stir through a few torn **Thai basil leaves**. Give it a taste and add more **Thai basil** until you're happy with the flavour. Fluff up the **rice** with a fork and share between your bowls. Top with the **pork** and get stuck in. Super tasty, or as the Thais say: 'Aloy mak!'

## Hello
## THAI BASIL

*It may take a little bit of hunting to find Thai basil but it's worth the effort. It has an aniseedy vibe to it that really makes this recipe come alive.

# GREEK LENTIL & LAMB RAGU
## – WITH HOMEMADE MINTY TZATZIKI –

**READY IN 35 MINS**  **SERVES ②**

There is a satisfaction in creating something from scratch that needs to be experienced to be truly appreciated. Especially when making it yourself is cheaper, fresher, additive-free and of course more delicious than buying pre-made. That's what tonight's tzatziki is all about. The cherry on top? This particular version comes with an extra large helping of bragging rights.

### Ingredients

- 1 onion, thin half moons
- 1 garlic clove, finely chopped
- 2 tbsp fresh mint leaves, finely chopped
- 3 tbsp flaked almonds
- 250g lamb mince
- olive oil
- 1½ tsp dried oregano
- 1½ tsp ground cumin
- 1 cinnamon stick
- 50g red split lentils, rinsed
- 1 tin chopped tomatoes
- 1 chicken stock pot
- 100g cracked bulgur wheat
- ½ cucumber, grated
- 100g Greek yoghurt
- ½ lemon, zest and juice
- salt and black pepper

### Here's how...

**1** Prep the **onion** and **garlic**. Pick the **mint leaves** from their stalks and finely chop (discard the stalks).

**2** Heat a frying pan over a medium–high heat with no oil, add the **flaked almonds** and fry until golden brown. Watch them closely as they love to burn when your back's turned.

**3** Once the **almonds** are put to one side, put the pan back over a medium–high heat. Add the **lamb mince** to the pan (again with no oil) along with ½ tsp **salt** and a few grinds of **black pepper**. Use a wooden spoon to break the **mince** up and cook until brown, 5 mins. When the **mince** is browned, add the **onion**. Stir together and cook until soft (add 1 tsp **oil** if the pan is dry), 5–6 mins. Then add the **dried oregano**, **cumin** and **cinnamon stick**. Stir together and cook for 1 min more.

**4** Rinse the **lentils** then add to your pan along with the **tomatoes** and half the **chicken stock pot**. Pour in 200ml water, bring to a gentle boil and put a lid on. Bubble away gently over a medium heat for 10–15 mins with the lid on until the liquid has reduced by half and the **lentils** are soft, stirring occasionally. If the mixture is looking a little dry, just add a splash more water. Once cooked, taste and add a bit more **salt** and **black pepper** if you feel it needs it.

**5** Put a saucepan of 200ml water over a medium heat with the remaining half **chicken stock pot** and stir to dissolve the **stock pot**. Add the **bulgur wheat** and bring to the boil. When boiling, cover with a lid, take off the heat and leave to rest for 15 mins.

**6** To make the **tzatziki**, cut the **cucumber** in half lengthways (no need to peel), remove the seeds by dragging the tip of a teaspoon through the middle and discard. Grate it on the coarse side of your grater. Put the **grated cucumber** in a small bowl and mix in the Greek yoghurt, lemon zest, garlic and half the **mint**, season with ½ tsp **salt**, a few grinds of **black pepper** and add the **lemon juice** to taste.

**7** Fluff up the **bulgur wheat** with a fork and stir in 1 tbsp **olive oil** and the remaining **mint**. Serve in bowls with the **lamb ragu** on top (don't forget to remove the **cinnamon stick**), a good spoonful of **tzatziki** and a sprinkle of **toasted almonds**.

# – SUPER –
# MEXICAN SHEPPY PIE

🕐 **READY IN 45 MINS**                    **SERVES** ② 

We're not sure if Mexicans have their own version of our Shepherd's Pie, but we're going to guess that if they did, this would be it. People are often curious about what chefs eat when they're at home and for me this is an absolute favourite. We highly recommend making a double or triple portion so you have plenty to eat on the day and the day after.

## Ingredients

- 600g sweet potato, 2cm dice
- olive oil
- 1 green pepper, 1cm dice
- 1 carrot, ½cm dice
- 1 onion, thin half moons
- ½ chilli (more if you like it hot), deseeded and finely chopped
- 250g beef mince
- 1½ tbsp fajita spice mix (or generic Mexican spice mix)
- ½ beef stock cube
- 1 tin chopped tomatoes
- 1 tbsp tomato purée
- 1 ball mozzarella
- 150ml soured cream
- salt and black pepper

## Here's how...

**1** Preheat your oven to 220°C/Gas Mark 7. Wash and chop your **sweet potato** into 2cm dice (no need to peel). Toss the wedges in 1 tbsp **olive oil** and ½ tsp **salt**. Lay them flat on the baking tray and roast on the top shelf of your oven for around 25 mins, or until a little crispy at the edges.

**2** Prep the **green pepper, carrot, onion** and **chilli**.

**3** Heat 1 tbsp **olive oil** in a frying pan over a medium–high heat. Add the **beef mince** and break it up with a wooden spoon. Cook for 2 mins without stirring. Turn and cook for another 2 mins without stirring. Leaving the **mince** alone allows it to get really brown, improving the taste. Remove the **mince** and set aside on a plate.

**4** Put the (now empty) pan back over a medium–high heat with another 1 tbsp **olive oil**. Add the **onion, pepper, chilli** and **carrot** with ¼ tsp **salt**. Cook for 6 mins.

**5** Add the **fajita** (or **Mexican**) **spice**, ½ tsp **salt** and a good grind of **black pepper**. Next add the ½ **beef stock cube**, the **tomatoes, tomato purée** and the browned **mince**. Allow to simmer and thicken until there is almost no liquid left, about 15 mins.

**6** Once the **sauce** has thickened, pour into an ovenproof dish. Top with the roasted **sweet potato** and tear over the **mozzarella**. Place on the top shelf of your oven and bake until the **mozzarella** has melted, 8–10 mins. When golden, remove from the oven and serve with the **soured cream**.

# SUPER-QUICK CREAMY PASTA
## – WITH PEAS & BACON –

🌓 **READY IN 30 MINS**　　　　　　　**SERVES** ②

There are more important things in life than spending hours toiling in the kitchen on a weeknight. Like putting your feet up on the sofa with a blanket and a cuppa or working on your Scrabble game. That was the motivation behind this comforting little number. This one is a quickie, so less time cooking and more time perfecting your triple word score.

### Ingredients

- **1 onion**, ½cm dice
- **2 garlic cloves**, finely chopped
- **1 courgette**, ½cm dice
- **3 tbsp fresh flat leaf parsley**, roughly chopped
- **5 rashers streaky bacon**, cut into 1cm pieces
- **olive oil**
- **200g fusilli**
- **60g frozen peas**
- **150ml crème fraîche**
- **40g Parmesan**, grated
- **salt and black pepper**

### Here's how...

**1** Put a large pan of water with 1 tbsp **salt** over a high heat and bring to the boil for the **pasta**. Prep the **onion**, **garlic**, **courgette** and **parsley**. Cut the **bacon** into 1cm pieces (you might find it easier to do this with scissors, just don't forget to wash them up properly).

**2** Put a frying pan over a medium–high heat with 1 tbsp **olive oil**. Add your **bacon** and cook until it starts to crisp, around 4–5 mins. Remove from the pan (but leave the **oil**) and place it on some paper towel to soak up any excess **oil**. Reduce the heat to medium, add your **onion** and **courgette** and allow them to cook gently until soft, 6–7 mins. Add your **garlic** and cook for 1 min more.

**3** Meanwhile, add the **fusilli** to the boiling water and cook for 9 mins (or according to the packet instructions), until 'al dente' (cooked through but with a tiny bit of firmness left in the middle). For the last 3 mins add in the **frozen peas** to cook them too. Drain but keep some of your **pasta water** as you may need it for your sauce.

**4** While your **pasta** is cooking return your attention to the **sauce**. Add your **bacon** back into the pan with the **courgette** and **onion**, along with the **crème fraîche**, ¼ tsp **salt** and a few good grinds of **black pepper**. Give it all a good stir and heat until piping hot.

**5** Add the drained **pasta** to the **sauce**. Grate in half the **Parmesan** and give it all a really good toss in the pan to make sure the **pasta** is nicely coated in the **sauce**. Add a splash of the reserved **pasta water** if you feel it needs a little more liquid.

**6** Divide the **pasta** between your bowls, top with some **parsley** and grate over the remaining **Parmesan**.

# ORZO RISOTTO
## – WITH CHORIZO & BABY SPINACH–

🕐 **READY IN 35 MINS**                    **SERVES** ②

*Ingredients*

- 1 onion, 1cm dice
- 2 garlic cloves,
  finely chopped
- 1 tbsp fresh thyme
  leaves, finely chopped
- 220g cherry tomatoes,
  halved lengthways
- 60g chorizo, 2cm dice
- olive oil

- 2 tbsp tomato purée
- 200g orzo pasta
- 1 vegetable stock pot
- 1 ball buffalo mozzarella
- 50g Parmesan, grated
- 125g baby spinach
- salt and black pepper

We've always been about taking the intimidation factor out of new ingredients. When your eye scans across the various pasta choices it's easy to fall back on familiar spaghetti and penne, but the other shapes hide a whole world of texture and possibility. Orzo is a rice-shaped pasta and for this recipe you'll be using it like a risotto rice. Velvety and more-ish, say hello to your new favourite.

*Here's how...*

**1** Preheat your oven to 200°C/Gas Mark 6. Prep the **onion**, **garlic** and **thyme**. Cut the **cherry tomatoes** in half lengthways. Cut the **chorizo** into 2cm dice.

**2** Put the **tomatoes** on a baking tray, add 1 tsp **olive oil**, season with ¼ tsp **salt**, a few grinds of **black pepper** and roast on the top shelf of your oven for 10 mins. Once cooked, remove from the oven and set aside.

**3** Put the kettle on to boil. Heat 1 tbsp **olive oil** in a large saucepan over a medium heat. Add the **onion** and season with ¼ tsp **salt** and a few grinds of **black pepper**. Stir and cook until soft, 5 mins. Next add the **garlic**, **thyme**, **tomato purée** and **chorizo** to your pan. Give everything a good stir. Cook for another 2 mins. Add the **orzo** to the pan and stir again so it gets a good coating of all the other ingredients.

**4** Pour 500ml boiling water into the pan along with the **vegetable stock pot**. Stir to dissolve the **stock pot**. Simmer, stirring occasionally to ensure nothing sticks to the bottom of the pan, until the liquid has been absorbed and the **orzo** is tender, 9–10 mins. If the liquid is all absorbed before the **orzo** is cooked, add another splash of water and give it a couple more mins.

**5** While the **orzo** cooks, roughly tear the **mozzarella** cheese into small pieces and grate the **Parmesan**. When the **orzo** is ready, take the pan off the heat, add the **mozzarella**, half the **Parmesan** and the **roasted tomatoes**. Stir gently. Add the **baby spinach** on top and pop a lid on the pan so the **spinach** wilts, 3–4 mins, then stir it gently together.

**6** Serve your **orzo** in bowls with the remaining **Parmesan** sprinkled on top.

# GLOBE-TROTTING BEEFBURGERS

## – WITH RED ONION MARMALADE –

🕐 **READY IN 40 MINS**   **SERVES** ②

Some people call them holidays, but I call them 'recipe reconnaissance missions'. This time my trip was deep into the Atlas Mountains of Morocco to spend time with the nomadic Berbers and learn about their food and their way of life. On my way back into Marrakech I passed an incredible riad where the food inspired this simple, delicious Moroccan-style burger. In fact, that trip inspired a whole Moroccan theme through the HelloFresh menu and justified numerous other 'missions'.

### *Ingredients*

- 1 red onion, thin half moons
- 500g potatoes, 2cm wedges
- olive oil
- 1 tbsp balsamic vinegar
- 250g beef mince
- ¾ tbsp ras-el-hanout
- 2 brioche buns
- 100g Greek yoghurt
- 50g baby leaf spinach
- salt and black pepper

### *Here's how...*

**1** Preheat your oven to 220°C/Gas Mark 7. Prep the **onion**. Wash and chop your **potatoes** in half lengthways (no need to peel). Rest the flat part on a board and slice into each half lengthways and at an angle to make 2cm thick wedges. Toss the wedges in 1 tbsp **olive oil**, ½ tsp **salt** and a grind of **black pepper**. Lay them flat on a baking tray and roast on the top shelf for around 25 mins, or until a little crispy at the edges.

**2** Put 1 tbsp **olive oil** in a small saucepan over a low heat. Add the **onion** and season with ¼ tsp **salt** and a few grinds of **black pepper**. Add the **balsamic vinegar** and place a lid on the pan. Cook gently for 20 mins, stirring once in a while.

**3** Put the **beef mince** in a mixing bowl. Add ½ tsp **salt** and the **ras-el-hanout** (this can be pretty spicy so add less if you don't like it hot). Form the **beef** into two equal-sized burger patties. They should be ever so slightly wider than your **buns**, as they'll shrink back when you cook them.

**4** Put 1 tbsp **olive oil** in a non-stick frying pan over a medium heat. Once hot, gently lay in the **burgers**. Cook for 5–6 mins. Turn and cook the other side for 5–6 mins. If you want to cook the **burgers** a little more in the middle, you can place them in your oven for a few mins after frying.

**5** When the **potato wedges** are 2 mins from being ready, lay the **brioche buns** on top of them to warm through. When warm, split open and pop in the **burgers** to serve.

**6** Serve your **burgers** with a spoonful of the **red onion relish** and the **Greek yoghurt**. Arrange some **potato wedges** and a handful of **spinach** leaves on the side.

# SOMETHING
## – FOR THE –
# WEEKEND

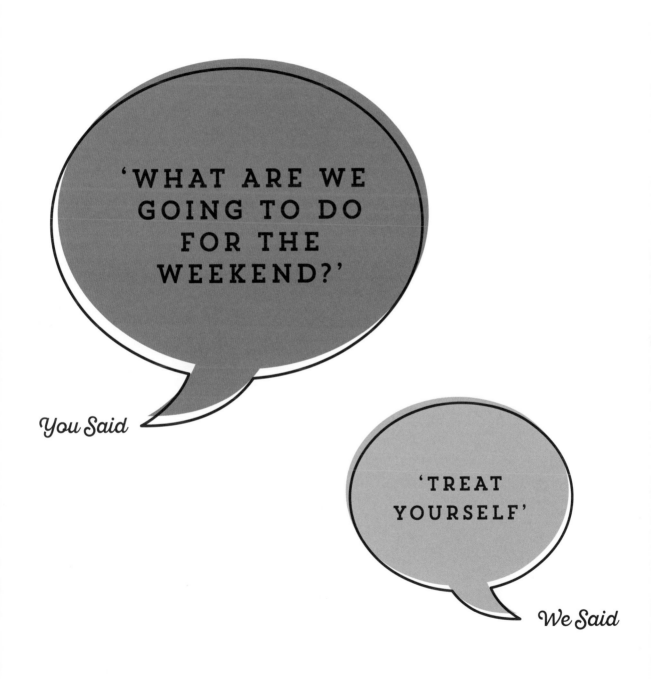

# – A HIGHLY DEBATED –
# FISHERMAN'S PIE

⏱ **READY IN 45 MINS**                    **SERVES** ②

The perfect Bloody Mary, the best cheeseburger, the tastiest fishermen's pie: there are certain dishes that invite endless comparison and debate. When we sent this one out, everybody weighed in with their tips on tweaking it to perfection and this is the result. Double or triple the ingredients and it's perfect for the family to dive into at the weekend.

## Ingredients

- 500g potatoes, peeled and cut into 3cm dice
- 1 leek, 1cm discs
- 2 tbsp fresh flat leaf parsley, finely chopped
- 40g Cheddar, grated
- 1 fish stock pot
- olive oil
- 100g green beans, trimmed
- 60g butter
- 50g flour
- 350g seafood mix*
- 100g frozen peas
- 3 tbsp milk
- 25g panko breadcrumbs
- salt and black pepper

## Here's how...

**1** Put a large pan of water with ½ tsp **salt** over a high heat and bring to the boil. Peel and prep your **potatoes** and put them into the water. Cook for 10–15 mins, or until you can easily slip a knife through them. Drain and leave in the pan until later.

**2** Prep your **leek**, **parsley** and **Cheddar**. Boil a kettle of water and dissolve your **stock pot** in 650ml boiling water.

**3** Heat 1 tbsp **olive oil** in a large frying pan over a low heat and fry the **leeks** with ¼ tsp **salt** and a few grinds of **black pepper** for up to 8 mins until they are completely soft. Don't let them brown. Trim the ends from your **green beans** and discard the ends. Put a new pan of water with ½ tsp **salt** over a high heat and bring to the boil for your **green beans**.

**4** Remove your **leeks** from the pan and add three-quarters of your **butter** to the pan. Once melted, add the **flour**. Stir together to form a smooth paste and gently cook for 2 mins before adding a quarter of your **fish stock**. Stir until smooth and then gradually add the remaining **fish stock** whilst stirring. Gently cook for 5 mins or until you have a thick, gravy-like consistency. At this point stir in your **leeks**, **seafood** and **peas** and leave for a further 5 mins, then remove from the heat. While the sauce is cooking, cook the **green beans** for 1–2 mins in the boiling water. Drain them and then immediately run them under cold water to stop them cooking (i.e. 'refresh' them).

**5** With your **filling** resting off the heat, it's **mash** time. Put the remaining **butter** in with the **potatoes** and put the pan back over a low heat. Add the **milk**, ½ tsp **salt** and, using a potato masher or the back of a fork, mash it for all you're worth.

**6** Check the seasoning in your **filling** and add a bit more **salt** and **black pepper** if needed. Stir through the **parsley** and pour the **filling** into an ovenproof dish. Top it with your **creamy mash**, followed by the **breadcrumbs** and **Cheddar**. Put under your grill on a high heat for 3–4 mins until golden and crunchy on top. Serve at the table with the **green beans** on the side and sail away!

Hello
SEAFOOD

*You can use a mixture of
salmon, cod, haddock,
mussels…go with your faves.

# – HOMEMADE VEGETABLE & CHORIZO PACKED –
# SMOKEY CALZONE

**READY IN 35 MINS**     **SERVES** (2)

'Cal-zone-ay' might sound a bit cheffy, but it's really just an Italian-style Cornish pasty.* For a while we'd been trying to figure out the best way to teach people dough-making, but then we discovered The Northern Dough Company, run by the lovely Amy and Chris. You can buy their delicious fresh dough in the supermarket and have all the fun of rolling it out and topping it. It's homemade without the hassle. Sounds like an ad for them, but in all honesty they totally deserve the credit!

*Don't tell the Italians we said that as there'll be trouble.

### Ingredients

- ½ red onion, 1cm dice
- 1 red pepper, 3cm dice
- 1 leek, 1cm discs
- 250g cherry tomatoes, halved lengthways
- olive oil
- 60g chorizo, ½cm dice
- 1 tbsp flour
- 2 balls ready-made pizza dough*
- 2 tbsp tomato purée
- 1 ball mozzarella
- 1 tsp Italian herbs
- 60g salad leaves
- salt and black pepper

### Here's how...

**1** Preheat your oven to 200°C/Gas Mark 6. Prep the **onion**, **pepper** and **leek**. Cut the **cherry tomatoes** in half lengthways.

**2** Place all your veggies on a baking tray and coat in 1½ tbsp **olive oil**, just over ¼ tsp **salt** and a few good grinds of **black pepper**. Cook on the top shelf of your oven for 20 mins.

**3** Chop your **chorizo** into ½cm **dice**. Heat 2 tsp **olive oil** in a frying pan over a medium heat and, once hot, add the **chorizo**. Cook for a few mins until slightly crisp at the edges, then take the pan off the heat.

**4** Dust your work surface with the **flour**, roll out the **pizza dough** into rounds, roughly 25cm across, and place on a lightly oiled baking tray. **Tip: If you don't have a rolling pin you can always use a wine bottle wrapped in clingfilm, or even a tin can.**

**5** Spread the **tomato purée** thinly over each pizza base, leaving a border of around 3cm at the edge.

**6** Once your **veggies** are soft, remove from your oven and divide them between each pizza base (making sure you only cover one half of each base, so you can fold the other half over). Be careful not to add any excess water from the vegetables to prevent the pizza base getting soggy. Tear the **mozzarella** on top of your **veggies** and sprinkle over the **chorizo** and **Italian herbs**. Turn your oven to maximum temperature.

**7** To make your **calzone**, run a wet finger around the border of each **pizza base**, then fold over and press the edges down to seal. Cook on the top shelf of your oven for 8–10 mins, until just browned. Serve with **salad leaves** on the side (we used **rocket**).

## Hello
# ITALIAN PASTY

*If you've got a bit of time then you can also make the dough at home the day before. It's worth looking at a recipe on YouTube so you can see the technique in action.

# CHICKEN MILANESE
## – WITH ROASTED NEW POTATOES & CHIVES –

**READY IN 30 MINS**                    **SERVES** ②

I love how the Italians can make something rather basic sound so sophisticated. In the UK we would call this recipe 'Chicken in Breadcrumbs', but 'Milanese' makes it sound like a dinner party speciality. The dish actually dates back at least as far as the 12th century and although it's often served alongside spaghetti in tomato sauce, we're mixing it up a little bit.

### Ingredients

- 450g new potatoes, halved lengthways
- olive oil
- 2 skinless chicken breasts, flattened
- 100ml soured cream
- ½ tsp garlic salt
- ½ lemon, zest and juice
- 50g panko breadcrumbs
- 3 tbsp fresh chives, finely chopped or snipped
- 60g salad leaves
- salt and black pepper

### Here's how...

**1** Preheat your oven to 220°C/Gas Mark 7. Wash the **new potatoes** and cut in half lengthways (no need to peel). Toss the **potatoes** in 1 tbsp **olive oil**, ½ tsp **salt** and a few grinds of **black pepper**. Lay them flat on a baking tray and roast on the top shelf for around 25 mins, or until a little crispy at the edges.

**2** Sandwich each **chicken breast** between two pieces of clingfilm. Bash the **chicken** with the bottom of a saucepan until it is ½cm thick all over.

**3** Put most of the **soured cream** (save 1 tbsp) into a mixing bowl and add the **garlic salt** and a few grinds of **black pepper**. Grate in the **lemon zest** and mix well. Put the **breadcrumbs** in another mixing bowl. Thoroughly coat each flattened **chicken breast** with the **soured cream** mix. Then transfer to the second bowl and coat in **breadcrumbs**, patting them onto the **chicken** to make sure they stick.

**4** Put 1½ tbsp **olive oil** over a medium heat in a non-stick frying pan. Carefully place the **chicken** in the pan. Cook until the **breadcrumbs** are golden and the **chicken** is cooked through, around 5 mins on each side (you may need to add a little more oil when you turn them over). Resist the temptation to move them around or they won't crisp up properly. The **chicken** is cooked when it is no longer pink in the middle.

**5** Make a **dressing** with the remaining **soured cream**, the **lemon juice** (add 1 tsp at a time, depending on how citrussy you like it) and 1 tbsp **olive oil**. Snip a sprinkling of **chives** into the **dressing** as well. Mix really thoroughly with a bit of **salt** (less than ¼ tsp) and a few grinds of **black pepper**.

**6** Gently toss your **salad leaves** in the **dressing** just before serving (not earlier as the leaves will go soggy). Snip the rest of the **chives** over your **potatoes** and serve everything straightaway.

# SHEPHERD'S PIE

🕐 **READY IN 40 MINS**          **SERVES** (2)

André has put a twist on an old favourite with this recipe by adding a hint of Middle Eastern-style spice to a traditional shepherd's pie. He's also leaving the skins on the potatoes for the mash. Not just because it's quicker and easier – they're full of nutrients and fibre, too. So, less work + more goodness = double win.

*We get ours from seasonedpioneers.com but if you can't get hold of any then try Bart's baharat spice mix.

## Ingredients

- 700g potatoes, 2cm dice
- 250g lamb mince
- ½ red onion, ½cm dice
- 1 garlic clove, finely chopped
- 1½ tsp shawarma spices*
- 220ml tomato passata
- 1 chicken stock cube
- 3 tbsp Cheddar, grated
- 1 tbsp butter
- 3 tbsp milk
- 200g tenderstem broccoli
- olive oil
- salt and black pepper

## Here's how...

**1** Put a large saucepan of water with ½ tsp **salt** over a high heat and bring to the boil. Chop the **potatoes** into 2cm dice (no need to peel) and add them to your pan of boiling water. Cook for 20 mins until tender and you can easily slip a knife through them. When done, drain in a colander. Set aside for 2 mins to let the steam escape, then return to the pan (off the heat) to keep warm.

**2** Put a frying pan over a high heat and add the **lamb mince** (no oil necessary). Brown the **mince**, breaking it up with a wooden spoon as it cooks. Prep the **onion** and **garlic**. Once the **mince** has browned, drain any excess fat and add the **onion**. Give it a stir and lower the heat to medium. Cook for 4–5 mins.

**3** When the **onion** is soft, add the **garlic** and the **shawarma seasoning**. Cook for 2 mins. Next, add the **tomato passata**, **chicken stock cube** and 4 tbsp water. Stir well to dissolve the **stock cube** and simmer until the **lamb** mixture has thickened and reduced by half, 10–15 mins. Grate the **Cheddar** and pop another large saucepan of water on to boil for your **broccoli**. Preheat your grill to its highest setting.

**4** When the **potatoes** are cooked and drained, mash with a potato masher or the back of a fork and mix through the **butter** and **milk**. Season with ½ tsp **salt** and a few grinds of **black pepper**. Taste the **lamb** mixture and add more **salt** and **pepper** if necessary. Spoon the **lamb** mixture into an ovenproof dish. Top with the mashed potato, then sprinkle over the **Cheddar**. Pop the dish under your grill until the **cheese** is golden and bubbly, 3 mins.

**5** Cook the **tenderstem broccoli** in your pan of boiling water, 3–4 mins. Drain into a colander, then season with **salt** and **black pepper** to taste.

**6** Share the **shepherd's pie** between your plates with the **broccoli** on the side.

# CONFIT DUCK LASAGNE

🕐 **READY IN 40 MINS**　　　　　　　**SERVES** ②

Here at HelloFresh HQ we've always referred to ourselves as a family. But that's not to say there isn't a very healthy sense of competition between family members, especially the chefs. When we were putting this book together it originally included a duck confit tagliatelle which we were pretty darn proud of. That was until Mimi swooped in with this lasagne. Hats off Mimi, you got this one!

## *Ingredients*

- 2 confit duck legs*
- 1 tin chopped tomatoes with garlic and onion
- ½ chicken stock cube
- 1 tbsp butter
- 1 tbsp white flour
- 250ml milk
- 20g fresh basil, stalks and leaves
- 60g Parmesan, grated
- 150g egg lasagne sheets
- 150g tenderstem broccoli
- olive oil
- salt and black pepper

## *Here's how...*

**1** Boil your kettle and **preheat your oven to 200°C/Gas Mark 6**. Peel the skin off the **confit duck legs** using your fingers and discard (it's a bit messy, but hey ho). Pull the **duck flesh** off the bone then use two forks to pull the **flesh** apart into very fine shreds (like you'd see in a Chinese restaurant).

**2** Put the **duck** into a frying pan over a medium heat and pour in the **chopped tomatoes**. Add 75ml water and the ½ **chicken stock cube** and turn the heat to medium. Grind in some **black pepper** and bring to a simmer, stirring to dissolve the **stock cube,** then allow to simmer until thickened, 10 mins. Stir occasionally. Remove from the heat.

**3** Meanwhile, to make the **béchamel sauce**, melt the **butter** in a saucepan over a medium heat, then add the **flour**. Stir together and cook (continuing to stir) for 2–3 mins. Pour in a third of the **milk** and stir or whisk together while the mixture comes to the boil; it should thicken as it comes to the boil. Pour in the remaining **milk** and whisk together again until the sauce boils and thickens again. Remove from the heat and season with ¼ tsp **salt** and a few grinds of **black pepper**.

**4** Roughly chop the **basil** (**stalks** and **leaves**) and stir into the **duck ragu** once it has thickened. Spoon a third of the **ragu** into an ovenproof dish in an even layer, then drizzle over a third of the **béchamel sauce**. Sprinkle over a third of the **Parmesan**. Cover with a **lasagne sheet**, making sure it is the right size for your dish (just snap it to make it the right size if not).

**5** Repeat step 4 with the next third of **ragu, béchamel** and **Parmesan** and a **lasagne sheet**. Top with the remaining **ragu**, then **béchamel** and sprinkle on the remaining **Parmesan**. Bake on the top shelf of the oven until you can easily stick a knife through the **pasta** and the top is golden, 25 mins.

**6** Put the **tenderstem broccoli** on a baking tray and drizzle with 1 tbsp **olive oil**, ¼ tsp **salt** and a few grinds of **black pepper**. When the **lasagne** has been cooking for 15 mins, put the **broccoli** in your oven for the last 8 mins of **lasagne** cooking time. Serve on plates with a side of crispy **tenderstem broccoli**.

## Hello
## CONFIT DUCK LEGS

*Granted you don't see these everywhere but they're worth tracking down for this recipe. A quick search online should do the trick.

# COURGETTE PARMIGIANA
## – WITH INSALATA CAPRESE –

🕐 **READY IN 40 MINS**　　　　　**SERVES** ②

*Ingredients*

- 1 red onion, ½cm dice
- 2 garlic cloves, finely chopped
- 2 courgettes, ½cm lengthways slices
- 150g cherry tomatoes, halved lengthways
- 2 balls buffalo mozzarella
- olive oil
- 1½ tsp dried oregano
- ½ tsp chilli flakes (optional)
- 500g tomato passata
- 50g hard Italian cheese (i.e. veggie Parmesan), grated
- 30g panko breadcrumbs
- 100g ready-made green pesto
- 3 tbsp pine nuts
- 1 ciabatta
- 1 tbsp fresh basil leaves, roughly chopped
- salt and black pepper

Sharing is caring and nowhere is this truer than here at HelloFresh. As with all the recipes in this book, the quantities are given for two portions, but everything is easily doubled and tripled. If you are going to make this parmigiana I'd really recommend doubling up the portion size, as there's hardly any added effort. Then you can share it around, or just keep a couple of portions for lunch the next day. I'd take the second option. Shhh.

*Here's how...*

**1** Preheat your oven to 190°C/Gas Mark 5. Prep the **onion** and **garlic**. Cut the **courgettes** lengthways into ½cm slices and cut the **cherry tomatoes** in half lengthways. Cut 1½ of the **mozzarella** balls into thin (½cm) slices and tear up the other half. Pat the **mozzarella** slices with some paper towel to soak up as much moisture as possible.

**2** Heat 1 tbsp **olive oil** in a frying pan over a high heat. Fry the **courgette** strips in batches for 1 min on each side, then set aside. Don't overcrowd the pan as this will stew the **courgette** rather than brown it.

**3** Meanwhile, put 1 tbsp **olive oil** in another frying pan over a medium–low heat. Add the **onion**, **garlic**, **oregano** and **chilli flakes** (if you decide to go for the spicy vibe). Fry until the **onion** is soft, about 5 mins. Add the **tomato passata** and season with ½ tsp **salt** and a few grinds of **black pepper**. Let the mixture simmer for 5 mins, then remove from the heat. Mix together the **hard Italian cheese**, the **breadcrumbs** and 1½ tbsp **olive oil** in a small bowl and set aside.

**4** Put a third of the **passata mixture** in an ovenproof dish and spread it out to cover the bottom. Top this with a layer of **courgette** (use roughly half your **courgette** here as you're going to repeat this step). Next layer on the sliced **mozzarella**. Drizzle over half of your **green pesto** and add half the **pine nuts**.

**5** Spread on another layer of **passata mixture**, followed by the remaining **courgette**, **pine nuts** and the other half of the **pesto**. Finish with a final layer of **passata** and top your **parmigiana** with the **hard Italian cheese** and **breadcrumb** mixture. Bake on the top shelf of your oven for 15 mins. Slice the **ciabattas** in half and drizzle 1 tbsp **olive oil** on top. Place on a baking tray and when the **parmigiana** has 5 mins left to cook, put them in the oven to warm up.

**6** Tear up the fresh **basil leaves** and mix with the torn **mozzarella**. Put these in a mixing bowl with the **cherry tomatoes**. Add 2 tsp **olive oil** and season with ¼ tsp **salt** and some **black pepper** just before serving (so the **basil** doesn't wilt). When the **parmigiana** is ready, serve generous portions with the **salad** and **ciabatta** on the side.

# BEDOUIN CHICKEN TAGINE
## – WITH APRICOT, FLAKED ALMONDS & COOLING YOGHURT –

**READY IN 45 MINS**  **SERVES** (2)

I've never believed that good things come to those who wait. The best things come to those who go out and get them. But there's an exception to that rule: tagine. This is definitely one of those dishes that benefits from low and slow cooking. If you want to take the flavour up to another level then I'd even suggest making it the day before and keeping it in the fridge overnight. You'll have the Bedouins knocking on your door.

*Ingredients*

- 1 **onion**, thin half moons
- 1 **carrot**, 1cm dice
- 1 **garlic clove**, finely chopped
- 6 **dried apricots**, finely chopped
- 200g **sweet potato**, peeled and cut into 1cm dice
- 4 skinless, boneless **chicken thighs**, bite-sized pieces
- **olive oil**
- 1 tbsp **ras-el-hanout spice**
- 1 **red chilli**
- 1 **chicken stock pot**
- 150g **couscous**
- 2 tbsp **flaked almonds**
- 2 tbsp **fresh mint**, finely chopped
- 2 tbsp **fresh flat leaf parsley**, finely chopped
- 1 **lemon**, zest and juice
- 150g **natural yoghurt**
- **salt and black pepper**

*Here's how...*

**1** Prep the **onion**, **carrot**, **garlic** and **apricots**. Peel and dice the **sweet potato**.

**2** Chop the **chicken** into bite-sized pieces. Heat 1 tbsp **olive oil** in a pan over a medium–high heat and, once hot, add the **chicken** and season with ½ tsp **salt** and a few grinds of **black pepper**. Cook for around 5 mins until soft, then remove from the pan (but leave any juices).

**3** Turn the pan down to a medium heat and cook the **onions** and **garlic** until soft, about 5 mins. Add the **ras-el-hanout** and stab the whole **chilli** a few times (the more you stab it, the hotter the final dish will be) before adding to the pan. Fry gently for 1 min.

**4** Add the **stock pot** with 500ml boiling water to the pan together with the **chicken**, **sweet potato**, **carrot** and **apricots**. Season with ½ tsp **salt** and and few grinds of **black pepper**. Cover with a lid and cook over a medium heat for 10 mins, then uncovered over a medium–low heat for 15 mins, until thickened up.

**5** Boil 300ml water with ¼ tsp **salt**, add in your **couscous** and cover the pot with a lid. Take the pot off the heat and leave to rest for 5 mins. Be exact with the amount of water to prevent soggy **couscous**.

**6** Heat a frying pan over a medium–high heat with no oil, add the **flaked almonds** and fry until golden brown, then remove.

**7** Prep the **mint** and **parsley** and mix all of the **mint** and two-thirds of the **parsley** into the **couscous**. Grate in the **zest** from half of the **lemon** and add 1 tbsp **olive oil**, 2 tbsp **lemon juice** and mix with a fork to separate the grains.

**8** Mix the **yoghurt** with 1 tbsp **lemon juice**, ¼ tsp **salt** and a few grinds of **black pepper**. Remove the **chilli** and serve the tagine on a bed of **couscous** topped with the **flaked almonds**, the lemony **yoghurt** and the remaining chopped **herbs**. You can also add a **lemon wedge** to the plate if you want an extra squeeze of citrussy juice at the table.

# BACON-WRAPPED PORK TENDERLOIN
## – WITH PEPPERCORN SAUCE –

🕐 **READY IN 45 MINS**                    **SERVES** ②

This recipe hails from the very first year of HelloFresh. We were planning our Christmas box and the idea of 'pigs in blankets' got me thinking about this recipe. There are a few more moving parts to this recipe than your average dinner, but by now you are whipping your way through all the techniques so it'll be a doddle. Here's a tip: if you want really smooth mashed potato you can push the cooked potato through a fine mesh sieve before you mix it with hot butter and cream. Silky!

### Ingredients

- 500g potatoes, peeled and cut into 3cm dice
- 1 garlic clove, finely chopped
- 1 echalion shallot (the long one), ½cm dice (smaller if possible)
- 250g pork tenderloin
- 6 rashers streaky bacon
- olive oil
- 300g tenderstem broccoli
- 1 beef stock cube
- 1 tsp black peppercorns
- 75ml double cream
- 4 tbsp milk
- 2 tsp butter
- salt and pepper

### Here's how...

**1** Preheat your oven to 200°C/Gas Mark 6. Put a large pot of water with 1 tsp **salt** over a high heat and bring to the boil.

**2** Peel and prep the **potatoes** and cook in the boiling water for 10–15 mins (until you can easily slip a knife through them). Drain and leave to the side in the same pan.

**3** While your **potatoes** are cooking prep the **garlic** and **shallot**. On a separate board trim off any visible fat (the white bits) from the **pork tenderloin** and cut widthways into two roughly 125g pieces. If you have leftover **pork** you can make another portion or freeze it for another day. Season each piece with ¼ tsp **salt** and a few grinds of **black pepper**.

**4** Lay three rashers of **bacon** lengthways on the chopping board overlapping each other by ½cm. Lay one piece of **pork** across the **bacon** at the end closest to you and then roll it up. Repeat using the remaining **bacon** and **pork**. Heat 1 tbsp **olive oil** in a frying pan over a medium–high heat. Place the **pork** in the pan (seam side down first) and cook for 3–4 mins on each side to brown and seal the meat.

**5** Once you have browned the **pork**, put it on a baking tray and roast on the top shelf of your oven for 10–15mins, until cooked through and no longer pink in the middle.

**6** Boil another pot of water with ½ tsp **salt** for your **broccoli**. Take your (now empty) frying pan and turn the heat to low. Add the **garlic** and **shallot** and cook for 1–2 mins. If there isn't enough **oil** left from the **pork** then add 2 tsp **olive oil**. Add the **beef stock cube** along with 100ml water, turn the heat to high and allow the liquid to reduce by half. Turn the heat back to medium–low, crush the **peppercorns\*** and add these with the **cream**. Bubble for 2–3 mins or until you have a thick **sauce**.

**7** While this is bubbling away add the **broccoli** to the other pan of boiling water and cook for 4 mins before draining. Put the **potatoes** back onto a low heat, add the **milk**, the **butter** and ½ tsp **salt**. Mash until smooth. Slice the **pork** into 2cm thick slices and serve with your **potatoes** and **broccoli**. Add a generous amount of **peppercorn sauce** to serve.

# Hello
# PEPPERCORNS

*You can use a pestle and mortar to crush peppercorns or just whack them with the bottom of a saucepan on your chopping board.

# – PRINCE HARRY'S BIRTHDAY –
# CHICKEN PIE

🕐 **READY IN 40 MINS**                    **SERVES** ② 

It's no secret around the HelloFresh Farm that Mimi has a substantial soft spot for our red-headed royal. She's also a big fan of anything involving potatoes and cream, so given the chance to cook for the man himself, she'd make him this pie. A creamy chicken filling topped with potato slices and cheesy breadcrumbs. Mimi's positive it's good enough for a prince and hopes you like it too.

## Ingredients

- 450g potatoes, peeled and in 1cm discs
- 1 leek, thin half moons
- 1 stick celery, ½cm dice
- 150g chestnut mushrooms, 1cm slices
- 2 skinless chicken breasts
- olive oil
- 1 chicken stock pot
- 150ml double cream
- 50g Cheddar, grated
- 30g panko breadcrumbs
- 100g frozen peas
- salt and black pepper

## Here's how...

**1** Preheat your oven to 220°C/Gas Mark 6. Put a large saucepan of water with ½ tsp **salt** over a high heat and bring to the boil. Peel the **potatoes** and slice into 1cm discs. Prep the **leek** and **celery**. Cut the **mushrooms** into roughly 1cm wide slices. Cut the **chicken** into bite-sized pieces.

**2** Adjust the heat so your pan of water is only gently boiling. Put the **potatoes** into the water and cook until just soft and you can easily slip a knife through, about 10 mins. Be careful because you don't want the slices to break up too much. Once cooked, carefully drain in a colander.

**3** Heat 1 tbsp **olive oil** in frying pan over a medium–high heat. Add the **chicken**, season with ¼ tsp **salt** and **black pepper** and cook until the **chicken** is browned, cooked through and no longer pink in the middle, about 5–6 mins. Cook your **chicken** in two batches if necessary.

**4** Once cooked, remove your **chicken** from the pan. Add 1 tbsp **olive oil** and the **leek** and **celery**. Cook until slightly softened, 4 mins. Add the **mushrooms** along with ¼ tsp **salt** and a good grind of **black pepper**. Turn the heat up slightly and cook everything together until the **mushrooms** are slightly browned, about 5 mins.

**5** Pour in 100ml water and add the **chicken stock pot**. Bring to a boil and stir to dissolve the **stock pot**. Add the **cream** and bring back to a gentle boil, then turn down the heat and simmer gently until reduced by a third, 4 mins. Meanwhile, grate the **Cheddar** into a mixing bowl. Add the **panko breadcrumbs** and 2 tbsp **olive oil**. Stir together and put another pan of water over a high heat to come to the boil for your **peas**.

**6** Once the sauce has reduced, return the **chicken** to the pan. Taste and add **salt** and **pepper** if you think it needs it. Transfer the mixture to an ovenproof dish and top with the **potato slices**. Sprinkle over your **cheesy breadcrumbs**. Season with **black pepper** and bake on the top shelf of your oven until the top is golden brown, 10 mins. Meanwhile, add the **peas** to your boiling water and cook for 3–4 mins. Serve the **chicken pie** with the **peas** on the side.

# LAMB & PASTA BAKE

## – WITH ROSEMARY –

🌓 **READY IN 30 MINS**  **SERVES** ②

Two of our favourite customers, Leisa and Pastor Steve, always have a yearly cook-up for the local community, so Leisa and I always catch up over how to multiply a HelloFresh recipe to feed 150+ people. I love how all the HelloFresh cooks I meet have colour-coded files of all their favourite recipes and cook them time and again. Next time I speak to Leisa I'll be recommending this one – perfect for cooking a big batch and giving a tummy-full of happiness.

*Ingredients*

- 200g rigatoni pasta
- 250g lamb mince
- 1 red onion, ½cm dice
- 1 garlic clove, finely chopped
- 2 tsp fresh rosemary leaves, finely chopped
- olive oil
- 220ml tomato passata
- 1 chicken stock cube
- 120g baby spinach
- 40g Parmesan, grated
- 30g panko breadcrumbs
- 100ml crème fraîche
- salt and black pepper

*Here's how...*

**1** Put a large saucepan of water with 1 tbsp **salt** over a high heat and bring to the boil for the **pasta**. Put a frying pan over a high heat and add the **lamb mince** (no oil). Break it up with a wooden spoon and leave it relatively undisturbed to cook until well browned, about 5 mins. Drain off any excess fat.

**2** Prep the **onion, garlic** and **rosemary**. Add the **onion, garlic** and half the **rosemary** to the **lamb**. Rosemary is a strongly flavoured herb so add less if you're not a huge fan. Give it a stir and lower the heat to medium. Cook until the **onions** have softened, 4–5 mins.

**3** Put the **pasta** in your pan of boiling water. Cook until 'al dente' (cooked through with a bit of firmness left in the middle), about 11 mins (or according to the packet instructions). When cooked, drain in a colander and return to the pan off the heat. Drizzle over ½ tbsp **olive oil** to stop it sticking together while you make the sauce.

**4** Meanwhile, add the **tomato passata, chicken stock cube** and 150ml water to the **lamb mixture**. Bring to the boil and stir to dissolve the **stock cube**. Reduce the heat to a simmer and let the **sauce** thicken and reduce by half, 15 mins. Then add the **spinach**, stir through and cook until wilted. Preheat your grill to its highest setting.

**5** In a small bowl, mix the remaining **rosemary** with half the **Parmesan** and all of the **panko breadcrumbs**. Season with ¼ tsp **salt** and a few grinds of **black pepper** and stir in 1 tbsp **olive oil**. Set aside.

**6** Mix the **crème fraîche** and remaining **Parmesan** into the **pasta**. Spoon your **lamb mixture** into an ovenproof dish and top with the **creamy pasta**. Sprinkle the **breadcrumb** mixture on top and grill for 2–3 mins. You want the **breadcrumbs** to go golden brown but not burn, so watch them closely. Serve and savour immediately.

# SALMON EN CROUTE
## – WITH POPPY SEEDS & AVOCADO –

⏱ **READY IN 45 MINS**　　　　　**SERVES** ②

It wouldn't be unfair to say that if a HelloFresh recipe has either butter, cream or pastry in it, then it's probably one of Mimi's. You see Mimi very much subscribes to the little-bit-of-what-you-fancy-does-you-a-lot-of-good school of thought. If you want to pull out the stops for a dinner party then the smart money is most definitely on this one.

### *Ingredients*

- **2 leeks,** thin half moons
- **olive oil**
- **½ lemon,** zest and juice
- **3 tbsp fresh flat leaf parsley,** finely chopped
- **150g hot-smoked salmon,** flaked
- **1 tbsp wholegrain mustard**
- **100ml crème fraîche**
- **1 sheet (320g) all-butter puff pastry**
- **1 tbsp milk**
- **1 tbsp poppy seeds**
- **1 avocado**
- **1 tbsp honey**
- **40g baby salad leaves of your choice**
- **salt and black pepper**

### *Here's how...*

**1** Preheat your oven to 220°/Gas Mark 7. Prep the leeks. Heat 1 tbsp **olive oil** in a frying pan over a medium heat and cook the **leeks** along with ¼ tsp **salt** and a few grinds of **black pepper**. Stir together and cook until really soft and sweet, 8–10 mins.

**2** While the **leeks** are cooking, zest the **lemon** and finely chop the **parsley** (stalks and leaves). Peel any skin off the **hot-smoked salmon** and discard. Put the **salmon** in a mixing bowl and separate the flakes with two forks. Add the **lemon** zest, **parsley**, **wholegrain mustard**, ¼ tsp **salt**, a few grinds of **black pepper** and stir together.

**3** Once the **leeks** are soft, add to the **salmon mixture** and mix together, then stir in the **crème fraîche**. Taste the **mixture** (but don't eat it all) and add more **salt** and **pepper** if you feel it needs it. Unroll the **pastry**, halve it widthways and lay it on a piece of baking paper on a baking tray.

**4** Spoon the **mixture** onto half of one of the **pastry** pieces, keeping a 2cm border around the edge. Dip your finger in water and run it around the edge of the **pastry**. Fold the other half of the **pastry** over so the two edges meet. Squeeze the edges together then use a fork to seal them tightly. Use a sharp knife to prick a small hole in the top of the **pastry** (this lets the steam escape). Repeat with the other **pastry** piece.

**5** Brush the **pastry** with **milk**, then sprinkle over half the **poppy seeds**. Bake until golden brown, 18–22 mins. Meanwhile, slice the **avocado** in half lengthways and twist apart. Remove the stone, scoop out the flesh and chop into 2cm dice.

**6** To make the **dressing**, squeeze the **juice** of the half **lemon** into another mixing bowl and add the **honey**, remaining **poppy seeds**, 2 tbsp **olive oil**, ¼ tsp **salt** and a few grinds of **black pepper**. Mix together. Just before serving, add the **avocado** and **baby leaves** to the dressing and toss together. When the **salmon en croûte** is cooked, remove from the oven and carefully slice each one into two triangles. Serve with the **salad** on the side.

# ROASTED CHICKEN
## – WITH SMOKED PANCETTA & HERBED PUY LENTILS –

**READY IN 30 MINS**   **SERVES** (2)

If this dish were a place, it would be a rustic little cottage somewhere in the Provençal countryside. Puy lentils are often overlooked in favour of more conventional accompaniments, but when teamed with smoked pancetta and fresh herbs, they make the perfect bed for your crispy roasted chicken. If you happen to have a bottle of something Provençal in the wine rack then all the better. Bon appétit!

### Ingredients

- 4 skin-on, boneless chicken thighs
- olive oil
- 1 carrot, ½cm dice
- 1 onion, ½cm dice
- 1 stick celery, ½cm dice
- 2 tbsp fresh flat leaf parsley, finely chopped
- ½ tsp fresh thyme leaves, finely chopped
- 1 tin Puy lentils, drained and rinsed
- 100g diced pancetta
- ½ chicken stock cube
- 1 tbsp red wine vinegar
- 1 tsp cornflour, mixed with 1 tbsp cold water
- 1 bay leaf
- 100g green beans, trimmed
- salt and black pepper

### Here's how...

**1** Preheat your oven to 220°C/Gas Mark 7. Pat the **chicken** skin dry with some paper towel then rub ½ tsp **olive oil**, ¼ tsp **salt** and a few grinds of **black pepper** into each **thigh**. Place in a roasting tin and cook them in the oven on the top shelf for 20–25 mins until the skin is nice and crispy. Rest them out of the oven for 5 mins afterwards.

**2** Prep the **carrot, onion, celery** and **parsley**. Pick and chop the **thyme leaves**. Drain and rinse the **Puy lentils**.

**3** Heat 1 tsp **olive oil** in a frying pan over a medium–high heat and cook the **pancetta** until it is browned off. Remove the **pancetta** from the pan and keep it to the side for later. Place the pan back on the heat without washing it up and add the ½ **chicken stock cube, red wine vinegar** and 100ml water. Scrape all the lovely **pancetta** goodness up from the bottom of the pan. This is called deglazing. Mix together the **cornflour** and 1 tbsp water to make a smooth paste. When the sauce has bubbled away for 3 or 4 mins add the **cornflour** paste. Keep stirring while the **cornflour** thickens your sauce until it's lovely and glossy, then pour out and keep to one side.

**4** Turn the heat to medium–low, wipe out the pan with a paper towel and add 1 tbsp **olive oil**. Add the **carrot, onion, celery, bay leaf** and **thyme** along with ½ tsp **salt** and cook until nice and soft, about 5 mins. Whilst this is happening, put a medium pan of water with ½ tsp **salt** over a high heat and bring to the boil for your **green beans**.

**5** Add in the **pancetta** and the **Puy lentils** to the softened **vegetables**. Toss the ingredients together, season with ¼ tp of **salt** and a few grinds of **black pepper** and then turn off the heat.

**6** Cook the **green beans** for 1–2 mins in the boiling water. Drain them and then immediately run them under cold water to stop them cooking (i.e. 'refresh' them).

**7** Once the **chicken** is ready and rested for 5 mins (so that the juices can re-distribute evenly throughout the meat), reheat the sauce through and toss the **parsley** and the **green beans** into the **lentils**. Serve the **chicken** over the **lentils** with the **sauce** in a bowl on the side for people to pour over the top of the **chicken** at the table.

# CHIPOTLE STEAK
## – WITH SWEETCORN AND CRISPY POTATO HASH –

🕐 **READY IN 40 MINS**

**SERVES** ②

A useful tip for getting a nice golden brown crust on your steak is to pat each side dry with some kitchen towel before you season and oil it. Our other top tip is that once you've cooked it, let it rest out of the pan for a few minutes before you cut it. That way all the lovely juices redistribute throughout the meat, giving you a nice succulent finish. Perfection!

### Ingredients

- 450g potatoes, 2cm dice
- olive oil
- 1 red pepper, 2cm dice
- 1 echalion shallot (the long one), thin half moons
- 10g fresh coriander, roughly chopped
- 1 garlic clove, finely chopped
- 285g tin of sweetcorn, drained and rinsed
- 2 rump steaks
- 1 chicken stock pot
- 1 tsp chipotle paste
- 100ml crème fraîche
- salt and black pepper

### Here's how...

**1** Preheat your oven to 220°C/Gas Mark 7. Wash and chop the **potatoes** into 2cm dice (no need to peel). Toss the **potatoes** in 1 tbsp **olive oil**, ½ tsp **salt** and a few grinds of **black pepper**. Lay them flat on a baking tray and roast on the top shelf for around 25 mins, or until a little crispy at the edges.

**2** Prep the **red pepper, shallot, coriander** and **garlic**. Drain and rinse the **sweetcorn** in a sieve.

**3** Put a frying pan over a high heat (no oil). Add half the **sweetcorn** and cook until browned, 2–3 mins. Stir once only. Transfer to a bowl and repeat with the remaining **sweetcorn**. When done, add 1 tbsp **olive oil** to the (now empty) pan and lower the heat to medium. Add the **red pepper** and **shallot** and fry until softened, 5 mins. Add the **garlic** and cook for 1 min more. Return the **sweetcorn** to the pan and remove from the heat.

**4** Put another frying pan over a high heat. While it gets hot, rub each **steak** with ½ tsp **olive oil** and season with ¼ tsp **salt** and a few grinds of **black pepper**. Once the pan is very hot, lay in the **steaks** and cook for 2½ mins on each side, then remove to a board, cover with foil and rest. **Tip: We like our steak medium-rare but if you like yours medium, give them 2 mins more on each side.** Keep the **steak juices** in the pan as they'll add flavour to your **sauce** in the next step.

**5** Lower the heat to medium. Add 100ml water to the **steak-juice** pan with the **chicken stock pot** and half the **chipotle paste** (be careful, it's spicy). Stir to dissolve the **stock pot** and simmer until thickened, 2–3 mins. Add the **crème fraîche**, bring to the boil and then remove from the heat. Taste and add more **chipotle paste** if you like it hot.

**6** Reheat the **sweetcorn mixture** over a medium heat. When the **potatoes** are crispy, add to the pan and stir through the **coriander**. Season with **salt** and **black pepper** to taste. This is your **hash**. Slice the **steak** as thinly as possible. Share the **hash** between two plates, top with the **steak** and then drizzle over the **chipotle sauce**.

# PIZZA BURGERS
## – WITH HOMEMADE CHUNKY CHIPS –

🕐 **READY IN 40 MINS**　　　　　　**SERVES** ②

Our chef Lizzie isn't a fan of maths, but one sum has her very excited: pizza + burger = pizza burger. And judging by the comments that came through on our HelloFreshUK Facebook page when we sent this out, Lizzie could be on her way to a Nobel Prize. Check out her pro tip below for melting the cheese.

### Ingredients

- 250g beef mince
- 1½ tbsp Worcestershire sauce
- 1½ tsp Italian herb mix
- 450g potatoes, 2cm wedges
- olive oil
- 60g chorizo, ½cm slices
- 1 ball mozzarella
- 2 tbsp tomato ketchup
- 20g Parmesan, grated
- ½ cucumber, 1cm dice
- 2 vine tomatoes, 1cm dice
- ½ tbsp balsamic vinegar
- 2 brioche buns
- salt and black pepper

### Here's how

**1** Preheat your oven to 220°C/Gas Mark 7. Put the **beef mince** in a mixing bowl with the **Worcestershire sauce** and half the **Italian herbs**. Season with ½ tsp **salt** and a few grinds of **black pepper**. Mix together well then form into two equal-sized burger patties. They should be ever so slightly wider than your **buns**, as they'll shrink back when you cook them.

**2** Wash and chop your **potatoes** in half lengthways (no need to peel). Rest the flat part on a board and slice into each half lengthways and at an angle to make 2cm thick wedges. Toss the wedges in 1 tbsp **olive oil** and ½ tsp **salt**. Lay them flat on a baking tray and roast on the top shelf for around 25 mins, or until a little crispy at the edges.

**3** Cut the **chorizo** into ½cm slices. Cut two slices of **mozzarella** per person, about ½cm thick, and tear the rest into pieces. Put the **ketchup** in a small bowl and add half the **Parmesan** and the remaining **Italian herbs**. Quarter the **cucumber** lengthways and chop into 1cm dice. Chop the **tomatoes** into 1cm dice. Put the **balsamic vinegar** and 1 tbsp **olive oil** in another small bowl.

**4** Put 1 tbsp **oil** in a frying pan over a medium–high heat. When hot, carefully lay in your **burgers** and fry until browned all over, cooked through and no longer pink in the middle, carefully turning every 3–4 mins. This should take about 15 mins.

**5** When the burgers are almost done, carefully lay some **chorizo** on top of each followed by two slices of **mozzarella**. Sprinkle over the remaining **Parmesan**, then add 2 tbsp water to the pan and pop on a lid. Cook for 2–3 mins more. This creates steam which will melt the **cheese** and keep the burgers moist. Halve the **brioche buns** and put them in the oven, on top of the wedges, to warm.

**6** When everything is ready, spread some of the **herby ketchup** onto each half of the buns. Sandwich the **pizza burgers** between the **buns** and serve alongside plenty of **wedges**. For the salad just toss the **tomatoes**, **cucumbers** and **mozzarella** pieces in the dressing with ¼ tsp **salt** and some **black pepper**, then tuck in!

HelloFresh chefs, from left to right: Mimi Morley, André Dupin, Lizzie Arscott and Patrick Drake.

# INDEX

Greek lentil & lamb ragu with homemade minty tzatziki 192

homemade rocket pesto orzotto with charred courgettes & tomato salad 36

king prawn linguine with chilli & sun-dried tomato 130

lamb & pasta bake with rosemary 222

Mexican chicken & tomato jumble with nigella yoghurt 110

Middle Eastern spiced beef ragout with couscous, coriander & flaked almonds 184

mixed bean & pork chilli with brown rice & citrus soured cream 168

Moroccan-spiced salmon with lemon & caramelised onion couscous 128

Nick 'the knife' steak with rosemary roasted sweet potatoes 152

orzo risotto with chorizo & baby spinach 198

pan-fried sea bream with saffron mash 126

pizza burgers with homemade chunky chips 230

Rachel's italian pork & tomato risotto 172

roasted salmon with garlicky tomatoes & crushed potatoes 140

simply Simon's sumptuous sea bass with Thai tomatoes 124

a sneaky courgette & sun-dried tomato tart 74

speedy penne all'arrabbiata with fresh basil & parmesan 186

speedy rigatoni with cherry tomatoes & mozzarella 176

speedy Sicilian stew with herbed pork

& garlic ciabatta 156

spicy sausage chilli with homemade tortilla chips 188

super Mexican sheppy pie 194

sweetcorn fritters with avocado, tomato & feta 40

vegetable-packed tomatoey moussaka with cheat's garlic bread 70

**tortillas**

beef enchiladas with homemade ranchero beans 178

quickdraw quesadillas with tomato & corn salsa 50

rainbow pepper fajitas with homemade refried beans & citrus soured cream 42

spicy sausage chilli with homemade tortilla chips 188

**turkey:** gobble up turkey stir fry with rice 114

**tzatziki:** Greek lentil & lamb ragu with homemade minty tzatziki 192

**vegetables**

homemade vegetable & chorizo packed smokey calzone 206

lentil & vegetable hotpot with a cheese & potato topping 58

preparing & chopping 21–6

record-breaking chicken, chorizo & veg-packed 'paella' 88

'stress-busting' pan-fried chicken with creamy lentils 84

vegetable-packed tomatoey moussaka with

cheat's garlic bread 70

**walnuts**

garlicky prawns with proper mini roast potatoes & walnut parsley pesto 138

grilled salmon tarator with bulgur wheat tabbouleh 136

**yoghurt**

Bedouin chicken tagine with apricot, flaked almonds & cooling yoghurt 216

globe-trotting beefburgers with red onion marmalade 200

Greek lentil & lamb ragu with homemade minty tzatziki 192

Mexican chicken & tomato jumble with nigella yoghurt 110

spicy sausage chilli with homemade tortilla chips 188

tandoori-spiced aubergine with tomato & coriander rice & nigella yoghurt 62

**zest** 20

# ACKNOWLEDGEMENTS

So many people have poured their heart, soul and countless hours into building HelloFresh. They're a passionate, glass-half-full, entrepreneurial bunch who've made our fresh food mission a reality and who make this place such a fun place to work. Thanks to all of you beautiful humans for your indomitable spirit and especially to Dominik and Thomas for the vision that made all this possible.